Paul's Letter To Titus

Guidance for Twenty-First Century Churches

GUY MANUELL

ISBN 978-1-969865-42-8 (Paperback)
ISBN 978-1-969865-43-5 (ebook)

Dedicated to the memory of my parents, Jack and Lily Manuell, who first taught me that Jesus loves me.

Rise up! O men of God!
Have done with lesser things;
Give heart and soul and mind and
strength To serve the King of kings.

Rise up, O men of God!
His kingdom tarries long;
Bring in the day of brotherhood,
And end the night of wrong.

Rise up, O men of God!
The Church for you doth wait,
Her strength unequal to her task;
Rise up and make her great.

Lift high the Cross of Christ!
Tread where his feet have trod;
As brothers of the Son of Man
Rise up, O men of God!

William Pierson Merrill (1867-1954)

CONTENTS

PREFACE

This commentary looks backwards and forwards. It examines Paul's Letter to Titus (*Titus*) in its historical context, where the apostle provides guidance to his colleague, Titus, on the island of Crete as to what he needs to do to establish newly formed churches, founded because of an evangelistic mission by him and Paul. *Titus* is particularly concerned with the appointment of leaders for these churches and the qualifications that they must have. It also gives ample directions as to the behaviour of the Cretan Christians in general.

Additionally, this commentary looks forward from the first century AD to the letter's implications for the Church today concerning its leadership and the behaviour of Christians in general. As western society is quickly abandoning morality and social norms that have existed for centuries, it is relevant to ask whether these changes are having any effect on the Christian church. In my view, the answer is 'undoubtedly yes'. They are changes which, overall, are weakening the body of Christ on earth. This is why *Titus* needs to be taken seriously by the Church in the twenty-first century. Although written nearly two thousand years ago, Paul's advice to his colleague, Titus, about the essential elements of church leadership and its accompanying behaviour speak strongly as to how today's churches should be governed.

In a twenty-first century context *Titus* warns about a cancer that is ravaging the body of Christ. As with cancer in a human body, the cancer of liberal morality, theology and doctrine, based on a repudiation of the truth and validity of the Bible, must be identified and then excised ruthlessly with the sword of the Word of God. This is the only way that the body can be restored to health. Otherwise, the body of Christ will survive (cf. John 10:28) only as a broken reed (cf. Is. 42:3), rather than a tree firmly planted by streams of living water (cf. Ps. 1:3). The Church in the West is at a stage where radical surgery is essential. Even amputations of some leadership may be necessary if the body is to survive.[1]

Titus is generally bundled together with Paul's two letters to Timothy and the three are described as the 'Pastoral Epistles' ('PE'). Richard Phillips notes that 'the Pastoral Epistles drive stakes in the ground that outline a vital foundation for apostolic church structure and practice.'[2] However, a distinction can be drawn between the nature of *Titus* and the other two letters. 1 and 2 Timothy reflect Paul's pastoral concern and advice for his young apprentice, who would still have been a relatively young adult when he received the letters. On the other hand, Titus was a mature believer, having been associated with Paul for more than twenty years, being an adult when converted (cf. Gal. 2:1).

The predominant theme of *Titus* is not the pastoral needs of the recipient of the letter but pastoral instructions on the ordering of the Christian churches then existing on the island of Crete. To that extent, it is a pastoral letter but its nature is quite different to that of the Timothean letters, which gave guidance to Timothy himself. Therefore, if this differentiation is accepted, it is important to consider *Titus* as a different type of Pauline 'pastoral' epistle. It contains guidance which is still relevant to the ordering

1 The recent demise of the Archbishop of Canterbury is a case in point.

2 D. M. Doriani & R. D. Phillips, 2 *Timothy and Titus* (Phillipsburg, NJ: P & R Publishing, 2020), xv.

of churches today that seek to be faithful to biblical principles regarding their congregations, staff and worship.

In considering the Greek text, I have been aided by three exegetical summaries of *Titus*.[3]

Greenlee comments:

> When many commentaries are studied, it soon becomes apparent that they frequently disagree in their interpretations. That is the reason why so many answers in this book are divided into two or more interpretations. The reader's initial reaction may be that all these different interpretations complicate exegesis rather than help it. However, before translating a passage, a translator needs to know exactly where there is a problem of interpretation and what the exegetical options are.[4]

As far as twenty-first century churches and Christians are concerned, the Word of God is unchanging in its moral and ethical demands on humans in general, and God's people in particular. It is as though modern theologians and interpreters of Scripture believe that God changes His mind to suit current social and ethical whims, like woke ideology on gender, morality, and political philosophies. This is not so because God's views are unchanging. 'For I, the LORD do not change', (Mal. 3:6). Therefore, the principles enunciated by Paul to Titus (and Timothy) remain a solid foundation on which to build modern Christian communities (cf. 2 Tim. 2:19). Particular emphasis is laid on the characteristics of church leaders. They have the responsibility for the correct preaching of the gospel and the holy duty of church administration. *Titus* provides specific guidelines for success in this endeavour.

---

[3] J. H. Greenlee, *An Exegetical Summary of Titus and Philemon*, second ed. (Dallas, TX: SIL International, 2008); L. J. Perkins, *The Pastoral Letters: A handbook on the Greek text*. BHGNT (Waco, TX: Baylor University Press, 2017); M. Zerwick & M. Grosvenor, *An Analysis of the Greek New Testament*, vol. 2. (Rome: Biblical Institute Press, 1979).

[4] Greenlee, *Titus and Philemon*, 7.

I thank the staff of the Leon Morris Library, Ridley College, Melbourne for their willing assistance and especially my wife, Bernice, for her ongoing encouragement.

September 2025
Curlewis, Australia

ABBREVIATIONS FOR BOOKS OF THE BIBLE

Old Testament		*New Testament*	
Genesis	Gen.	Matthew	Matt.
Exodus	Ex.	Mark	Mark
Numbers	Num.	Luke	Luke
Deuteronomy	Deut.	John	John
1 Samuel	1 Sam.	Acts	Acts
2 Kings	2 Kings	Romans	Rom.
Ezra	Ezra	1 Corinthians	1 Cor.
Nehemiah	Neh.	2 Corinthians	2 Cor.
Psalms	Ps.	Galatians	Gal.
Proverbs	Prov.	Ephesians	Eph.
Ecclesiastes	Eccles.	Philippians	Phlp.
Isaiah	Is.	Colossians	Col.
Jeremiah	Jer.	1 Thessalonians	1 Thess.
Ezekiel	Ezek.	1 Timothy	1 Tim.
Daniel	Dan.	2 Timothy	2 Tim.
Joel	Joel	Titus	Tit.
Amos	Amos	Philemon	Phlm.
Haggai	Hag.	Hebrews	Heb.
Malachi	Mal.	James	Jas.
		1 Peter	1 Pet.
		2 Peter	2 Pet.
		Jude	Jude
		Revelation	Rev.

Abbreviations for Publications

AB	The Anchor Bible
BECNT	Baker Exegetical Commentary on the New Testament
BHGNT	Baylor Handbook on the Greek New Testament
BCBC	Believers Church Bible Commentary
BTCP	Biblical Theology for Christian Proclamation
BBC	Blackwell Bible Commentaries
ESV	English Standard Version
HNTC	Harper's New Testament Commentaries
HCSB	Holman Christian Standard Bible
HSIBD	*The Hodder and Stoughton Illustrated Bible Dictionary*
ICC	International Critical Commentary
IVPNTCS	IVP New Testament Commentary Series
KJV	King James Version
LXX	Septuagint (Old Testament in Greek)
MacNTC	The MacArthur New Testament Commentary
MNTC	Moffatt New Testament Commentary
NASB	New American Standard Bible, 1995
NASBEC	*The Strongest NASB Exhaustive Concordance*
NEB	New English Bible
NICNT	New International Commentary on the New Testament
NIV	New International Version
NKJV	New King James Version

NRSV	New Revised Standard Version
NT	New Testament
NTS	*New Testament Studies*
NT	*Novum Testamentum*
OT	Old Testament
PNTC	Pillar New Testament Commentary
SHBC	Smyth & Helwys Bible Commentary
TNTC	Tyndale New Testament Commentary
TDNT	Theological Dictionary of the New Testament
UBCS	Understanding the Bible Commentary Series
WBC	Word Biblical Commentary
ZECNT	Zondervan Exegetical Commentary Series on the New Testament

INTRODUCTION

Crete in the First Century AD

Crete is the fifth largest island in the Mediterranean Sea, lying to the south of Greece (see map below).[5] It now forms part of modern Greece. It is relatively long and narrow, stretching for 160 miles (260 km) on its east-west axis and varying in width from 7.5 to 37 miles (12 to 60 km) north to south. It is a particularly mountainous country through its interior. The apostle Paul first visited Crete on his voyage from Caesarea to Rome, where he would present his case to Caesar. Acts 27:6-12 provides a most realistic description of that voyage. Rather than being chained as a Roman prisoner, Paul visited Crete about three years later of his own volition with his longstanding Christian companion, Titus. It was to be a mission of evangelism. Since this time in Crete occurred after the chronological end of Acts, we have no record in the NT of what occurred, except from this letter of Paul to Titus.

[5] See reddit.com: A Map of Hellenistic Crete. *https://www.google.com/search?q=map+of+first+century+crete&rlz=1C1CHBF_en - GBAU865AU865&oq=map+of+first+century+crete&gs_lcrp=EgZjaHJvbWUyBggAEEUYOTIGCAEQRRhA0gEJMTI5M jdqMGo3qAIAsAIA&sourceid=chrome&ie=UTF-8#vhid=9a1ydESMV4iV3M&vssid=l*

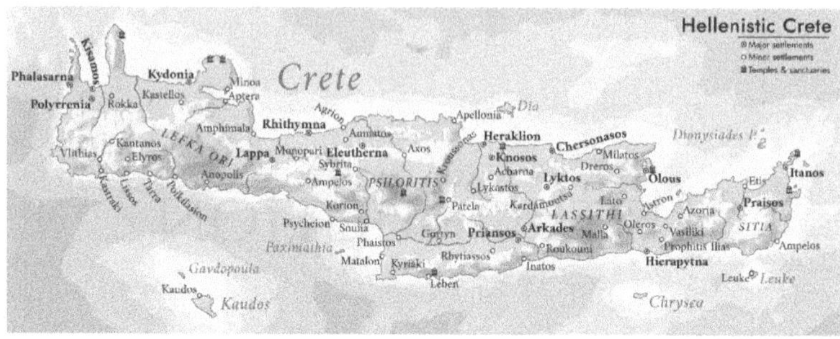

Crete's geographic location made it ideal for trade and piracy. 'One of the last strongholds to resist Roman domination, it finally came under Rome's sway and was made a province in 71 BC.' [6] From the contents of *Titus* (1:5, 12), and the opinions of many commentators, it seems clear that this letter was written by Paul and delivered to Titus on Crete. Yet, in a relatively recent article (2009) Weiland claimed that: 'The implied destination of the letter to Titus has long puzzled scholars. "Why Crete is chosen here", Houlden confesses, "is a mystery to us".' [7] Weiland refers to commentators M. Dibelius, H. Conzelmann, J. D. Quinn and L. Oberlinner as sharing this view. I regard Weiland's apparent puzzlement as bizarre and, like most commentators, assume that Titus received the letter while on Crete.

We do not know where Paul and Titus travelled on Crete or for how long, but it was sufficient for Christian churches to be formed in some towns.

The apostle Paul's charge to Titus is 'to appoint elders in every town (πόλις)' (1:5). A literate audience would be familiar with the statement by the famous classical poet Homer, who spoke of 'Crete of the hundred cities' (Homer, *Iliad* 2.649), no doubt by way of poetic hyper-

---

[6] P. H. Towner, *The Letters to Timothy and Titus*. NICNT (Grand Rapids: Eerdmans, 2006), 39-40.

[7] G. M. Wieland, 'Roman Crete and the Letter to Titus.' *NTS* 55:3 (2009): 338-54, 338.

bole. Along its extensive coastline, many of Crete's towns were connected by sea as well as roads but there is little evidence of a Roman road system.[8] This lack of infrastructure shows how ambitious Paul and his associates were in targeting the entire island and all its towns for evangelization. Thus, Titus was faced with a formidable challenge, both logistically and theologically (in view of the false teachers). During the Hellenistic period, some forty towns are known. There were many towns in Crete (see map) across difficult terrain.

> The issue is what would these πόλεις on Crete have been like in the mid-first century AD. Πόλις is rarely used in the New Testament epistles and would appear to be here identifying the urban, political units of the Roman provinces of Crete and Cyrenaica, which is how the term is used in the Greek world.
>
> The establishment of churches throughout the island is mirrored by events in the adjacent provinces of Achaea (Corinth), Macedonia (Philippi, Thessalonika), and Asia (Ephesus) where the major cities became the focus for evangelism.[9]

About twenty such towns are attested in the Roman period as issuing coins of their own and being administered by their own magistrates. The most prominent cities in the early Roman period were Gortyn (the administrative capital, known for its celebrated 'Gortyn Code,' a set of classical codified laws),[10] Knossos (a Roman colony most likely established by Augustus) famous for its Bronze Age

---

[8] I. F. Sanders, *Roman Crete: An Archaeological Survey and Gazetteer of Late Hellenistic, Roman and Early Byzantine Crete* (Warminster, UK: Aris & Phillips, 1982), 7.

[9] D. W. J. Gill, *A Saviour for the Cities of Crete* in P. J. Williams, A. D. Clarke, P. M. Head, D. Instone-Brewer (eds.), *The New Testament in Its First Century Setting: Essays on Context and Background in Honour of B. W. Winter on His 65th Birthday* (Grand Rapids: Eerdmans, 2004), 220.

[10] See comments on 3:13 regarding Zenas the lawyer.

palace, and the less-explored Eleutherna, Hierapytna, and Kydonia. Gortyn, the Roman capital located in the south of the island, was not far from the places Paul passed along the Cretan coast on his voyage to Rome.

When Paul and Titus first visited Crete it had many pagan religions, principally of Greek and Roman origin. At one time, Crete served as the centre of the Minoan civilisation (c. 2700–1420 BC), which many regard as the earliest recorded civilization in the continent of Europe. For those interested in biblical history, it can be noted that the OT enemies of Israel, the Philistines, originated in Crete (known as Caphtor) (cf. Gen. 10:14; Deut. 2:23; Jer. 47:4; Amos 9:7). In the first century AD, the cult of Augustus and Roma appears to have been practiced in Gortyn, while the cult of the deified Claudius is attested for Knossos. The cult of Asclepius, a god of healing, was confirmed in at least eighteen locations. The Egyptian cult of Isis and Serapis is attested as well. Under Tiberius (ruled AD 14–37), Crete was used for exiles from Rome (Tacitus, *Ann.* 4.21). In addition to the Roman administrators, a local leading official, the *Koinon*, organized quinquennial games and issued coins, seeking to maintain a distinct Greek identity. 'The second most popular cult was that of Asklepios [sic]; this is found in at least 18 locations across the island.'[11]

Paul often uses the term 'Saviour' in *Titus* (1:3, 4; 2:10, 13; 3:4, 6; cf. 1 Tim 1:1; 2 Tim 1:10). This may have attracted special attention from the Cretans, especially if Titus was located in Gortyn. An inscription from probably the second century AD was found at the sanctuary of Asclepius at Lebena (see Leben on map) south of Gortyn, reading, 'Diodorus dedicated to you, Saviour, two dreams in return for twofold eyes, light being restored.' Another similar Greek inscription, addressed to Zeus and

[11] Gill, *A Saviour for the Cities of Crete*, 227.

attributed to a Corinthian named Plotius, was found at Knossos. This evidence for the use of 'Saviour' pertaining to Greek deities provides a crucial backdrop for Paul's references to God and Jesus as 'Saviour', designating them as the true provider and exclusive mediator of salvation, respectively.[12]

There was also a Jewish community on Crete (cf. Acts 2:11) and Paul is critical of some of them who were Christians but did not want to abandon Jewish myths (cf. Tit. 1:10, 14). The Alexandrian Jewish philosopher Philo wrote in the early 40s AD that 'not only are the mainlands full of Jewish colonies but also the most highly esteemed of the islands, Euboia, Cyprus, Crete' (*Leg.* 282). The contemporary Jewish writer, Flavius Josephus, admitted to marrying a Cretan Jewess from a prominent family (*Life of Flavius Josephus*, 282).

Considering this background information, it is possible that Titus was based in or near Gortyn, the provincial capital, and that his task as apostolic delegate was to establish a body of elders in the churches of every one of the twenty or so cities on the island. As Wieland notes in his essay on 'Roman Crete', 'Gortyn is traditionally held to be Crete's first ecclesiastical centre, and it would not be surprising if a Christian mission located itself in such a leading town, nor that both recruits and opposition to the Christian movement should come from the Jewish community already established there.'[13]

From both a logistical and theological perspective, Crete would be a difficult nut for Titus to crack. No doubt, Paul realised this from his visit to the island. Unsurprisingly, therefore, Paul's letter to Titus begins and ends with 'grace'. The power of the Holy Spirit to

[12] This information on Crete in Roman times is excerpted and slightly adapted from A. J. Köstenberger, *1-2 Timothy & Titus*. Biblical Theology for Christian Proclamation (Nashville: B&H, 2017), 296–99 and Gill, *A Saviour for the Cities of Crete*.

[13] Wieland, 'Roman Crete and the Letter to Titus', 352-53.

strengthen and enlighten Titus is evident throughout the letter. The gospel would conquer the inherent social difficulties to be found among the Christians on Crete.

Who Was Titus?[14]

Titus was resident in Crete when he received Paul's letter. His is a Roman name meaning 'pleasant'.[15] Titus was one of Paul's most longstanding partners in the work of the gospel. He is mentioned in several of Paul's letters: Galatians, 2 Timothy and, especially, 2 Corinthians, but never in Acts.

Titus' relationship with Paul covered several decades, reflected in Paul's descriptions of him as 'my brother' (τὸν ἀδελφόν μου – *ton adelphon mou*) (2 Cor. 2:13); 'my partner and fellow worker' (κοινωνὸς ἐμὸς καὶ εἰς ὑμᾶς συνεργός – *koinōnos emos kai eis humas sunergos*) (2 Cor. 8:23)[16]; 'my true child in a common faith' (γνησίῳ τέκνῳ κατὰ κοινὴν πίστιν – *gnēsiō teknō kata koinēn pistin*) (Tit. 1:4). His conduct was beyond reproach (2 Cor. 12:18).[17] It has been argued that his omission from Acts reflects him being a relative of that book's author, Luke.

> Thus it may very well have happened that Luke was a relative of one of the early Antiochian Christians; and this relationship was perhaps the authority for Eusebius's carefully guarded statement. Further, it is possible that this relationship gives the explanation of the omission

---

[14] For a complete overview of Titus in the NT, see 'Titus' in G. Manuell, *The People in Paul's Letters: A Compendium of Characters* (Fearn: Christian Focus Publications, 2025), 338-45.

[15] *The Hodder and Stoughton Illustrated Bible Dictionary*, 1058.

[16] See R. P. Martin, *2 Corinthians*. WBC (Grand Rapids: Zondervan, 2014), 456–58.

[17] See M. J. Harris, *The Second Epistle to the Corinthians: A Commentary on the Greek Text* (Grand Rapids: Eerdmans, 2005), 890-91; C. G. Kruse, *2 Corinthians: An Introduction and Commentary*. TNTC (Downers Grove, IL: Inter-Varsity Press, 2015), 273.

> of Titus from *Acts*, an omission which everyone finds so difficult to understand. Perhaps Titus was the relative of Luke; and Eusebius found this statement in an old tradition, attached to 2 Cor. 8:18; 12:18, where Titus and Luke (the latter not named by Paul, but identified by an early tradition) are associated as envoys to Corinth. Luke, as we may suppose, thought it right to omit his relative's name, as he did his own name, from his history.[18]

There is no evidence to confirm this and I regard it as unlikely. Like Luke, Titus was a Gentile (Gal. 2:3).

Chronologically, Paul and Titus first encountered each other at the church in Antioch. This would have occurred around AD 46-48. From Acts 15 it would seem that Titus probably would have been in his twenties. Titus is first mentioned by Paul in Galatians 2:1–3 when he accompanied the apostle to Jerusalem for the Council (about AD 48) concerning the need for circumcision by Gentile believers. Critically, the Jerusalem Council decided that Titus did not need to be circumcised (Gal. 2:3).[19]

> Because Paul mentions Titus in a separate construction, συμπαραλαβὼν καὶ Τίτον (*symparalabōn kai Titon,* taking along also Titus) [Gal. 2:1], Titus is given special prominence here (Mussner 1988: 101). We do not know when Paul first encountered Titus (not mentioned in Acts), but in Tit. 1:4 Paul's calling him 'my true son in our common faith' may imply that Paul was instrumental in his conversion. Titus had an especially important role with the Corinthian church on Paul's third missionary journey (2 Cor. 2:13; 7:6, 13–14; 8:6, 16, 23; 12:18), but he may also have been known to the Galatians (R. Longenecker 1990: 47). Paul's reason for highlighting his presence at

---

[18] W. M. Ramsay, *St Paul the Traveller and Roman Citizen* (London: Hodder and Stoughton, 1942), 389-90.

[19] G. S. Duncan, *The Epistle of Paul to the Galatians*. MNTC (London: Hodder and Stoughton, 1934), 42-48 argues strongly that Titus *was* circumcised in Jerusalem but his conclusion is rejected.

> the Jerusalem Council becomes clear as the narrative progresses: he was a Greek, and the fact that he was not compelled to be circumcised is powerful evidence that Paul's law-free gospel was acknowledged to be correct (Gal. 2:3). In fact, it is possible that Paul brought Titus along to Jerusalem precisely for the purpose of forcing the issue (e.g., Hays 2000: 222; Garlington 2003: 71).[20]

Titus was clearly a close companion of Paul, as we see from 2 Corinthians 2:13. Paul had travelled to Troas (north-western Turkey) in the Roman province of Mysia expecting to meet Titus, who was travelling there with news of the Corinthian church. So great was Paul's desire to see Titus that he reluctantly left the infant church formed in Troas and travelled to Macedonia. When they met in Macedonia Titus was able to encourage Paul with a favourable report about affairs in Corinth (2 Cor. 7:6-7; cf. 2 Cor. 11:28).

> The agitation that troubled Paul's spirit and made his ministry at Troas less than it might have been is clear from this text. When pastoral concerns weighed heavily on him, he could not put his heart in evangelistic opportunity. In the event it was better for him to quit Troas and press on to meet his colleague on his return from Corinth. No good purpose is served, we learn, in any Christian's attempting a piece of service when his or her interests lie elsewhere; and pastoral responsibility stood high on Paul's agenda at this time.[21]

Paul's comments about meeting Titus are interrupted by a lengthy discourse in 2 Corinthians 2:14-7:4. Paul then resumes his comments about Titus, who was clearly of considerable influence in the Corinthian church as described

---

[20] D. J. Moo, *Galatians*. BECNT (Grand Rapids: Baker Academic, 2013), 122.

[21] R. P. Martin, *2 Corinthians*, 180. See Kruse, *2 Corinthians*, 116-17; Barnett, *2 Corinthians*, 134-36.

in 2 Corinthians 7-8. One word used several times by Paul to describe his fellow worker is 'earnest' (σπουδή–*spoudē* and its derivatives), defined in the *Compact Oxford English Dictionary* as 'sincere and serious about one's intentions'. Such was Titus' attitude towards the Corinthian church.[22] However, the use of σπούδασον (*spoudason*) in *Titus* also brings a sense of making haste to undertake this journey.[23] Paul had sent Titus to Corinth with the responsibility to deliver a severe letter to the church, calling it to repentance (2 Cor. 7:8–9). Paul had led Titus to believe that he would be welcomed by the Corinthian congregation and this indeed was the outcome.

> Paul also rejoiced when he saw how Titus' own heart now went out to the Corinthians: *And his affection for you is all the greater when he remembers that you were all obedient, receiving him with fear and trembling.* As Titus recalled their obedience (to the demands made in Paul's 'severe letter') and the fear and trembling with which they received him [Titus] (evidence of the respect in which they held Paul and his apostolic team), his affection for them increased. Their *fear and trembling* may also be evidence of an awareness of their failed responsibility before God, to whom they would have to give an account for the way they had acted during the crisis in Corinth. Informing the Corinthians of Titus' growing affection for them would predispose them to welcome him when he made his upcoming visit in the administration of the collection for the poor believers in Jerusalem.[24]

---

[22] See Harris, 2 *Corinthians*, 599–600. Matthew Henry used Titus' 'earnestness' as an exemplar in his *Sermon Preached at Haberdashers' Hall, 13 July 1712 on the Occasion of the Death of the Rev. Richard Stretton, M.A.* The word 'earnest' is used seventy-two times. See M. Henry, *The Complete Works of Matthew Henry: Treatises, Sermons, and Tracts*. 2 vols. (Grand Rapids: Baker Books, reprinted 1979), vol. 2, 384–402.

[23] See the use of σπούδασον in 2 Tim. 4:9, 21 where urgency is emphasised.

[24] Kruse, 2 *Corinthians*, 195 (original emphasis).

Titus' journey to Corinth (alluded to in 2 Corinthians 12:18) is difficult to determine chronologically. The letter to Titus was penned in AD 63 from Macedonia.[25]

> Paul urged Titus ((παρεκάλεσα (*parekalesa*), aorist tense of παρακαλέω (*parakaleō*), 'urge') and sent with (συναπέστειλα (*sunapesteila*), aorist tense of συναποστέλλω (*sunapostellō*)) him a brother (τὸν ἀδελφόν–*ton adelphon*). We note that παρακαλέω, 'urge', is found in both [2 Cor.] 8:6 and 12:18, and may be grounds for connecting the two verses mentioned as describing the same visit. Also it appears that the aorist tenses of 12:18 are genuine (as they are in 8:6), and thus we see another link between 8:6 and 12:18. What must remain a mystery is, if 8:6 and 12:18 describe the same visit, why did not Paul mention the brother in 8:6? Possibly at the time of writing 8:6, Paul did not deem it important to mention the identity of the other brother. This is possible in that Paul was not defending his action toward the offering when he composed chapters 1–9, while he was having to defend it in chapter 12. Whatever the reason, it seems more logical to equate 8:6 and 12:18. Moreover, the person of Titus is more important to Paul's argument. For one, Titus was a Gentile (no doubt an important item with the Corinthians). Furthermore, Titus had the confidence of the Corinthians. He had started the collection [for Jerusalem] in Corinth and had been the one to deliver the 'severe letter'. Whatever one's conclusion about 12:18a, Titus must be seen as playing a vital role in Paul's self-defence.[26]

Titus contains few references to Titus personally and is more in the form of written instructions about how Titus is to behave as a Christian in that difficult location (Crete) and build up the church there by appointing elders and teaching the believers how to behave. If Paul wrote to Titus around 63 AD, Titus would have been in his early forties, hardly a 'young man' (cf. Titus 2:6).

---

25 See *Time Between Two Roman Imprisonments* in the Introduction to Manuell, *The People in Paul's Letters*, 46-48.

26 R. P. Martin, *2 Corinthians*, 645; see Barnett, *2 Corinthians*, 589-90.

The final mention of Titus (2 Tim. 4:10) was written during the apostle's second imprisonment in Rome. Paul simply notes: 'Titus [has gone] to Dalmatia' (2 Tim. 4:10). Dalmatia was a Roman province located on the eastern Adriatic Sea in the southern part of Illyricum, where Paul had preached the gospel (Rom. 15:19). Nicopolis is a town in that region.[27] There are two quite different descriptions of Nicopolis as a winter location. Towner writes, 'Nicopolis was a busy port town on the western coast of Greece. It was actually known for its harsh winters'.[28] Yet Köstenberger writes, 'Nicopolis, the preeminent location for trade with Rome in western and northern Greece, was known for its mild climate. ... Nicopolis was more than 300 miles from Crete, a five-to-ten-day journey by ship'.[29] To add further confusion, Long (unhelpfully) comments that 'there were several places named Nicopolis; it hardly matters which one is meant here'.[30]

> Nicopolis lay on the northwest coast of Greece opposite the foot of Italy. 'I've decided to spend the winter there [not "here"]' indicates that Paul hasn't yet arrived in Nicopolis. So we don't know where he was at the time of writing this letter (but see Romans 15:19 for his presence, perhaps at this time, in Illyricum, a region north of Nicopolis). He'll send Artemas or Tychicus to replace Titus in Crete. Then Titus is 'to be diligent' to join Paul in Nicopolis. Paul's decision to spend the winter in Nicopolis favours that the commanded diligence includes Titus' coming before winter's onset. For sailing during winter, as Titus would have to do when leaving the island of Crete, was dangerous and usually avoided (see Acts 27 for Paul's recognition of

---

27 Barclay, *The Letters to Timothy, Titus and Philemon,* 265 notes that Nicopolis was in Epirus and was 'the best centre for work in the Roman province of Dalmatia'.

28 P. H. Towner, *1-2 Timothy and Titus.* IVPNTCS (Downers Grove, IL: InterVarsity Press Academic, 1994), 263.

29 Köstenberger, *1–2 Timothy & Titus,* 353.

30 Long, *1 & 2 Timothy and Titus,* 278.

> the danger involving Crete). So, the commanded diligence in a sending of Zenas the lawyer and Apollos is also likely to include action taken before winter's onset (cf. 2 Tim. 4:9, 21).[31]
>
> In the concluding section of *Titus* Paul discusses his immediate plans and crisis instructions - Tit. 3:12–14 … Paul urged Titus to make every effort to join him for the winter. Do your best, he wrote, to come to me at Nicopolis (a city founded by Augustus on the site of his camp after his victory over Mark Antony at Actium, 31 BC). Paul had decided to spend the winter there (v. 12a). A similar message would be sent to Timothy in Paul's final days (2 Tim. 4:9, 21). Paul may have used his winters to regroup, rethink, reconceive his mission. Apparently, Paul's plan was to send either Artemas (not mentioned elsewhere) or Tychicus to replace Titus in Crete, while Titus was temporarily in Nicopolis consulting with Paul.[32]

As is the case with so many faithful saints, we know nothing about Titus' final years; however, tradition has it that he died on Crete. The first church dedicated to Titus was in Gortyn, which also housed the metropolitan see of the island until its destruction by earthquake and the Arab transfer of the capital from Gortyn to Heraklion in AD 828. The Church of Saint Titus in Heraklion, is one of the most important monuments in the centre of town, set in a lovely square: *Agios Titos* [Saint Titus] *Square*.[33]

Paul's Situation

The Book of Acts 28:31 ends with Paul in custody in Rome for two years, yet 'preaching the kingdom of God and teaching concerning the Lord Jesus with all openness, unhindered.' Paul's activities before his second and final

---

31 R. H. Gundry, *Commentary on First and Second Timothy, Titus* (Grand Rapids: Baker Academic, 2010), 71.

32 Oden, *First and Second Timothy and Titus*, 165.

33 See *https://www.explorecrete.com/heraklion/en13-heraklion-saint-titus*.

imprisonment in Rome (while awaiting execution) (2 Tim. 4:6ff.) are unknown other than from some clues from his letters, *Titus* and 1 Timothy. The period between Paul's two Roman imprisonments could be a span of several years, during which time he could have accomplished journeys both to the west (Spain, as per his desire in Romans 15:24) and to the east (the Mediterranean region).

The following selection of quotations (from commentaries) reflect a plausible set of circumstances regarding the provenance of 1 Timothy and *Titus* and the chronology of Paul during this period.[34] I have no alternative regarding this aspect of Paul's life other than to turn to reliable scholars.

> These letters [Pastoral Letters] do not need to be fitted into the period covered by Acts because Acts did not record Paul's death. On the assumption that Paul was released from his Roman prison described in Acts, as he expected, his ministry continued, during which time the three letters were written; the last (2 Timothy) was written from his second Roman imprisonment immediately before his death (see Schlatter, pp. 232-39). Evidence for a second imprisonment was received as credible by Eusebius, who wrote in the fourth century: 'There is evidence that, having then been brought to trial, the apostle again set out on the ministry of preaching, and having appeared a second time in the same city [Rome] found fulfillment in martyrdom. During this imprisonment he composed the second Epistle to Timothy, referring both to his earlier trial and to his impending fulfillment' (Eusebius, 2.22.2, p. 96). Although we do not have the documentary evidence

[34] See Manuell, *People in Paul's Letters,* 56-63; B. Witherington III, *Letters and Homilies for Hellenised Christians: A Socio-Rhetorical Commentary on Titus, 1-2 Timothy and 1-3 John* (Downers Grove, IL: InterVarsity Press, 2006); T. C. Oden, *First and Second Timothy and Titus: Interpretation: A Bible Commentary for Teaching and Preaching* (Louisville: Westminster John Knox Press, reprinted 2012); J. R. W. Stott, *The Message of 2 Timothy.* TSBT (Leicester: InterVarsity Press 1973).

to which Eusebius referred, he had access to a splendid library at Caesarea. There is no extant tradition to the contrary.[35]

For these documents [the Pastoral Epistles] to be Pauline in any sense, they probably require that one presuppose that Paul was released from house arrest in Rome somewhere around AD 62, had a few further years of ministry, including on Crete and elsewhere in the east, then was taken prisoner again, and finally executed. In support of this suggestion is that 1 Clement 5:7 clearly tells us that Paul was released from his first captivity in Rome.

The following is a possible scenario that makes sense of the data that we find in the Pastoral Epistles, without placing them in a clearly post-Pauline context. First, we must theorise that Paul went to Crete with Titus and perhaps also Timothy for a period of time. Paul did the evangelistic tour of Crete but left Titus there to continue to make converts and organise the Christian house churches on the island that they had begun together.[36]

He [Paul] went to Crete where he left Titus behind (Titus 1:5), and then to Ephesus where he left Timothy behind (1 Tim. 1:3-4). He may well have gone onto Colosse to see Philemon, as he had planned (Phlm. 22), and he certainly reached Macedonia (1 Tim. 1:3). Of the Macedonian cities he visited, one will have been Philippi (Phlp. 2:24). From Macedonia he addressed his first letter to Timothy in Ephesus and his letter to Titus in Crete. He told Titus his intention to spend the winter at Nicopolis (Titus 3:12), a town in Epirus on the west (Adriatic) coast of Greece. Presumably, he did this, and Titus joined him there.[37]

The letter to Titus is the earliest of these three Pastoral Epistles, and probably it was written not from Rome, but rather from Macedonia. After leaving Crete, Paul went to Macedonia, but by way of Ephesus with Timothy, where he found things in bad straits. False teachers had begun to seriously undermine the gospel and the earlier Pauline work in that city and region. Paul thus banished

35 Oden, *First and Second Timothy and Titus*, 26.

36 Witherington, *Letters and Homilies for Hellenised Christians*, 65.

37 Stott, *The Message of 2 Timothy*, 17.

the two major troublemakers, but he had to move on to Macedonia, perhaps due to difficulties in Philippi. He then left Timothy behind in Ephesus to continue to put out the fires and re-establish things in western Asia, dealing with aberrations in both praxis and belief. The problems here were in various respects like those on Crete, which is not a surprise, since both locales were dominated by highly Hellenised Gentiles.

It must be kept steadily in view that by this point in time, whatever their natural temerity or ages, both Timothy and Titus had had some years of experience as Pauline coworkers, and thus presumably Paul needed to do no more than just remind these two of what they should teach. Perhaps it was the size of the problems and the opposition and the tasks at hand that was the real rhetorical exigence prompting the writing of Titus and 1 Timothy. These letters are indeed hortatory in character and meant to encourage these two men to be brave, stand firm, and carry out the pastoral work that they have been called and equipped to do.

It probably is the case that both *Titus* and then 1 Timothy were written in a short period of time of each other, for they are so similar in their diction and in some of their content. The similarity in content of *Titus* and 1 Timothy makes it exceedingly unlikely that these two letters were written to the same audience. It would appear that 1 Timothy was written in Macedonia, while the letter to Titus was still rather fresh in Paul's mind. It could be argued, since Paul mentions no scribes in these two letters, that he himself wrote these documents, but it is possible that both Paul and Luke were involved in their composition. Paul does not always mention his scribes in his letters. I suggest these letters were written in AD 64-65, thus well over a year after the last of the Captivity Epistles (Philippians) was written from Rome in AD 62, just before Paul's release from house arrest.[38]

Paul expected Titus to leave Crete and come and winter with Paul on the west coast of Greece in Nicopolis

[38] Witherington, *Letters and Homilies for Hellenised Christians*, 65-66.

in the winter of AD 64-65. They could not have anticipated the firestorm that would fall on Christians because of the fire in Rome in AD 64. From this point on, Paul's movements become less clear, but it appears from these documents that Paul, after he had visited various of his other churches in Greece, returned after that winter to Asia, where he was taken prisoner, perhaps in Troas. This might have come not long after the fire in AD 64, but more likely in AD 65, when the Neronian crackdown on Christians and especially their leaders had gotten underway. Paul seems to have been done in by Alexander, who bore witness against him, leading to his being taken prisoner and carted off to Rome.

Three factors need to be considered. First, these are Paul's only truly personal and, indeed, private letters. They are not composed for oral delivery to a congregation,[39] and so while they do reflect rhetorical devices of various sorts, Paul is engaging in encouragement and exhortation rather than offering extended arguments and proofs – although, there are simple 'proofs' in 2 Timothy (alone). These arguments, however, are brief and largely paraenetic in character, and they serve more as reminders than as full-fledged attempts to convince, since Paul is preaching to the choir. In Titus and 1 Timothy the form of argument is more succinct and simpler and takes the form of brief rhetorical syllogisms or enthymemes, paradigms, rhetorical comparison (*synkrisis*), maxims and the use of traditional or sacred materials. Full formal arguments were not required to remind two of his coworkers what they needed to preach and teach and do.

We are told plainly at 2 Tim. 4:11 that Luke was with Paul at the time when he spoke the things now recorded in 2 Timothy. In addition, in my previous study of Acts, I pointed out that the "We" passages found in Acts 16:10-17 and in the latter part of the book do refer to the author of the document accompanying Paul on part of his second missionary journey, and his third, indeed accompanying

[39] However, W. D. Mounce, *Pastoral Epistles*. WBC. (Grand Rapids: Thomas Nelson, 2000), 385 comments that the tone of *Titus* suggests that it would have become a public document.

> him to Jerusalem and then on to Rome. I noted how the 'We' portions of the second missionary journey begin in Troas and end in Philippi.
>
> This is not unimportant to our discussion here, because Philippi in particular seems to be the city from which *Titus* and 1 Timothy were written. In my Acts commentary I noted that it would appear that Luke was an itinerant doctor, his normal orbit being back and forth across the Aegean between Troas and Philippi. It is perfectly plausible that Paul had reconnoitred with Luke again in Philippi, Luke helped him to write these first two letters, then travelled with Paul eventually on to Rome and helped him with the final letter as well. This last letter may have been written right at the end of Paul's life and sent just before his demise. Luke, of course, was a trusted companion of Paul, and one who had a Hellenistic style of writing. He may well be the only Gentile among the authors of the New Testament, and all the evidence cited above either comports with or points in the direction of Luke as a contributor to these letters. Luke then composed this letter for Paul, based on Paul's last oral testimonies and instructions while under restricted house arrest (perhaps in the Campus Martius, on the edge of Rome, where military prisoners were kept until trial), and perhaps he had before him one or the other of the previous two Pastoral Epistles, which he used as model for the composition of 2 Timothy in terms of phraseology and general style, and some content. Luke may have made copies of these documents when he wrote them for Paul in Macedonia.[40]

The above comments and conclusions provide clear guidance as to Paul's travels after his first Roman imprisonment and the location of his correspondence to Timothy and Titus in Philippi, Macedonia.

---

[40] Witherington, *Letters and Homilies for Hellenised Christians*, 66-68.

Commentary on Titus

CHAPTER 1

The Author's Salutation

1:1 *Paul, a bond-servant of God and an apostle of Jesus Christ, for the faith of those chosen of God and the knowledge of the truth which is according to godliness,*
1:2 *in the hope of eternal life, which God, who cannot lie, promised long ages ago,*
1:3 *but at the proper time manifested, even His word, in the proclamation with which I was entrusted according to the commandment of God our Saviour,*
1:4 *To Titus, my true child in a common faith: Grace and peace from God the Father and Christ Jesus our Saviour.* NASB

'Titus begins with one of the longest, and most complex, salutations of the canonical Pauline corpus.'[41] Paul's salutation to Titus must be recognised as a greeting to an individual, not a Christian church. Reflective of the letter's purpose to instruct Titus as to how he was to organise churches on Crete, it is analogous in form to the directions from a superior to junior officer in the Lord's army.

---

[41] J. Twomey, *The Pastoral Epistles through the Centuries*, Blackwell Bible Commentaries (Chichester: Wiley-Blackwell, 2009), 190. The salutation to Titus contains 65 words, whereas salutations in Galatians and Romans contain 75 and 93 words, respectively.

Nevertheless, the tone of the letter indicates that it was intended for 'public dissemination'.[42] The authority of the letter depends not on the content of the message but the authority of the sender. Reflecting the importance and urgency of the letter, it vindicates Paul's position as an apostle of Jesus Christ and his mission to the Gentiles (cf. 2 Cor. 4:5). However, it also contains a personal greeting to one his closest associates.

> What is striking about the salutation to Titus is its considerable differences from those in 1 and 2 Timothy, especially its lengthy elaboration of Paul's apostleship (vv 1–3), a phenomenon found elsewhere only in Romans. These verses, which form a single, extremely complex sentence in Greek, conclude with a note about his apostleship as a trust. The main thrust, however, emphasises the purpose of that apostleship: to bring God's people to faith and truth, and thus to life. That life, he explains, was promised by God before time began but has only now been revealed—through Paul's preaching.[43]

The opening salutation of *Titus* is the longest of Paul's personal letters to Timothy, Titus and Philemon. Like Romans, Paul describes himself as both slave and apostle (cf. 2 Pet. 1:1). As well as declaring Paul's apostolic authority, these four verses also introduce themes that will be developed later in the letter. Key words are 'eternal life' in 1:2; 3:7 (αἰώνιος ζωή - *aiōnios zōē*); 'faith' in 1:1, 4, 13; 2:2, 10; 3:15 (πίστις - *pistis*); 'godliness' in 1:11; 2:12 (εὐσέβεια - *eusebeia*); 'hope' in 1:2; 2:13; 3:7 (ἐλπίς - elpis); 'Saviour'/'salvation' in 1:3, 4; 2:10, 11, 13; 3:4, 5, 6 (σωτῆ - *sōtē*/σωτῆρος - *sōtēros*).

> Paul is looking back and looking forward. He is looking back on his ministry and trying to distil its essential core.

42 Mounce, *Pastoral Epistles*. 385.

43 G. D. Fee, *1 & 2 Timothy, Titus*, Understanding the Bible Commentary Series. rev. ed. (Grand Rapids: Baker Publishing Group, 2011), 167.

And he is looking forward to the ministry of those who will succeed him to give them a pattern to follow. This is what it is to be at the heart of gospel ministry – and so this letter provides us with an opportunity to recalibrate our lives and the lives of our churches.[44]

1:1 in Detail

παῦλος δοῦλος θεοῦ
Paul, a slave of God

The writer of this letter is the apostle, Paul, who was then located in Philippi, Macedonia. Like his other letters (Rom. 1:1; Gal. 1:10; Phlp. 1:1; Col. 4:12; 2 Tim. 2:24; cf. 1 Cor. 7:22-23), Paul describes himself as a *slave* (δοῦλος – *doulos*). It is important in this context to note that Peter, James (the brother of Jesus) and Jude all used the δοῦλος self-description (2 Pet. 1:1; Jas. 1:1; Jude 1) at the beginning of their letters. This is clearly a common understanding amongst Jesus' earliest followers.[45]

A lengthy explanation of the rationale for this 'slave' nomenclature is provided in *The Letter of Jude*.[46] The self-description of Jude in that book corresponds exactly to the thoughts of Paul in his use of δοῦλος regarding himself. A summary of Paul's rationale (from the *Jude* text) follows.

---

[44] T. Chester, *Titus for You* (UK: The Good Book Company, 2014), 14-15.

[45] In Rev. 15:3 Moses is described as ὁ δοῦλος τοῦ θεοῦ (cf. 1 Pet. 2:16). In this context the title 'Saviour' may have had some favourable influence with Jews on Crete. See J. MacArthur, *1-2 Timothy and Titus*. The MacArthur New Testament Commentary (Chicago: Moody Publishers, 1996), 4; Perkins, *The Pastoral Letters*, 243.

[46] G. Manuell, *The Letter of Jude: A Wake-Up Call to Twenty-First Century Christians*. rev. ed. (Sydney: Tulip Publishing, 2022), 70-75.

A slave was the lowest position that a person could occupy in first-century society. There can be no doubt that most slaves in the Roman Empire were regarded as, and treated as little better than, animals; like animals, slaves were subject to the complete power of their masters. It could be argued that, having come from the glory of the Father to life as a Nazarene carpenter, Jesus himself displayed the elements of utter debasement. This would be demonstrated in the extreme (especially for the Jews) by His dying on a cross. Nevertheless, there were many slaves who occupied positions of responsibility and authority within wealthy Roman households.[47]

Jude uses δοῦλος simply to reflect the position of the most subservient people in his society. That is his understanding of his relationship to Jesus the Christ[48] ... The slave's entire existence was determined by the master's will – for good or ill. As a slave of Christ, Jude is also subject to the will of his master, who will determine his role in life and control (own) his whole being. In Jude's case, his master will control what happens to the slave in life and death. ... Unlike earthly equivalents, this slavery is not forced on Jude. It is a (low) status placed on him by God, to which he voluntarily and willingly submits because he wants to be wholly owned and directed by the One who died for him.[49]

Jude's second premise for describing himself as a slave is the status of the master of the slave.[50] Slaves in a prestigious Roman household enjoyed the status of their master. Better to be a slave in Caesar's palace than one in rural Tuscany. But Jude is a slave of Jesus Christ! There could be no higher honour than to be a member of Christ's

---

47 Manuell, *Letter of Jude*, 73-74. See J. D. Quinn, *The Letter to Titus*, The Anchor Bible (New Haven, NJ: Yale University Press, 1990), 60-61 for the significance of δοῦλος in first century pagan religions and throughout the OT.

48 See M. J. Harris, *Slave of Christ: A New Testament Metaphor for Total Devotion to Christ*. New Studies in Biblical Theology 8 (Downers Grove, IL: Inter-Varsity Press, 1999).

49 Manuell, *Letter of Jude*, 73.

50 See Harris, *Slave of Christ*, 135.

> household (the King of kings), no matter how menial the duties (cf. Ps. 84:10). Given the nature of Christ (2 Cor. 10:1), it is absurd to regard the slave nomenclature as a reflection of base existence and ill treatment in a Christian context. On the contrary, slaves of Christ will eventually reign with him (Rev. 20:6). This is a future for which no earthly slave could ever hope, let alone attain.[51]
>
> [t]he correct translation of δοῦλος is 'slave', not euphemisms like 'servant' or 'bond- servant', which entirely misrepresent both the relationship described and the intention of the author. Note the frequent use of 'servant' (διάκονος - *diakonos*) in the NT to differentiate a servant from the lowlier designation of slave (cf. Matt. 25:14-30.)[52] Mistranslations of δοῦλος attempt to minimise the servitude of Jude (or Paul), whereas they wish to glory in their lowly position.[53]

There is an unusual feature to Paul's slave description in this letter. In all the references cited above, Paul describes himself as a slave of Jesus Christ but, in this instance, he calls himself a slave *of God*. The explanation probably resides in his next phrase, but it would have also resonated with Jews given his claim to be a slave of Yahweh (Jehovah).

ἀπόστολος δὲ ἰησοῦ χριστοῦ
and an apostle of Jesus Christ

Notwithstanding the close spiritual and personal relationship between Paul and Titus, this letter has a degree of formality between these Christian colleagues. Therefore, Paul states his credentials at the start of his letter, to use a

51 Manuell, *Letter of Jude*, 75.

52 See Harris, *Slave of Christ*, 135. P. H. Davids, *The Letters of 2 Peter, Jude*. PNTC (Grand Rapids: Eerdmans, 2006), 34-35 usefully notes that, when Jesus is referred to as 'servant of the Lord', in Acts 3:13; 4:27, 30, not δοῦλος but παῖς (*pais*) is used for 'servant', v 20. Harris makes the same point, at greater length, in Appendix 3.

53 Manuell, *Letter of Jude*, 75.

military analogy, in a manner that reflects a superior officer instructing a junior officer of his future responsibilities. He is Paul, a *slave of God* and an *apostle of Jesus Christ.*[54] Although Paul is a slave of God (the Father), he was commissioned in his apostleship by Christ after the incident on the road to Damascus. This slave/apostle description is evidence of both his commitment to divine control and to emphasise his authority as a messenger from Christ to direct Titus as to what he should do in Crete on behalf of the gospel.[55] The 'father/son' relationship (v 4) is also relevant to Paul's style of instruction to Titus.[56] The use of δὲ (*de* - and) 'indicates a more specific designation of Paul's office: God's slave: specifically, an apostle.'[57]

Paul reminds Titus that he has been commissioned by Christ Himself to proclaim the gospel and make disciples 'of all nations' (Matt. 28:19). This includes the Gentiles to whom Titus is ministering. As with his other letters, Paul uses 'of Jesus Christ' (ἰησοῦ χριστοῦ - *Iēsou Christou*) (1:1; 2:13; 3:6) and 'of Christ Jesus' (χριστοῦ ἰησοῦ - *Christou Iēsou*) (1:4) interchangeably in *Titus.*[58]

κατὰ πίστιν ἐκλεκτῶν θεοῦ
for the sake of the faith of those chosen of God

---

[54] Perkins, *The Pastoral Letters,* 243 notes that the connective δὲ (*de*) could be translated 'and at the same time'.

[55] 'This phrase is added because the situation addressed, like that of many of his letters, requires his authority as an apostle. It is an appropriate term in an official letter.' J. H. Greenlee, *An Exegetical Summary of Titus and Philemon.* second ed. (Dallas, TX: SIL International, 2008), 13. See also Fee, *1 & 2 Timothy, Titus,* 167; J. N. D. Kelly, *A Commentary on the Pastoral Epistles.* Harper's New Testament Commentaries (London: Adam & Charles Black, 1963), 226-27.

[56] See Chester, *Titus for You,* 41-42.

[57] Greenlee, *Titus and Philemon,* 13.

[58] In all his letters, Paul uses ἰησοῦς χριστός (*Iēsus Christos*) seventy-seven times and χριστός ἰησοῦς (*Christos Iēsus*) eighty-two times. There appears to be no specific reason for the order of the words.

κατὰ can have two meanings here. One is 'for' and the other 'according to' (cf. 2 Tim. 1:1). Why was Paul an apostle? The better sense seems to be that he had a ministry to lead to faith those chosen by God. The purposefulness of 'for' seems the preferable translation. It might be extrapolated to mean 'for the benefit of'; 'in the interest of'. The RSV translation has 'to further the faith of God's elect', which well describes Paul's appointment as an apostle. It was for a specific purpose: to enhance the faith of believers. 'Faith' is mentioned in vv 1, 4. 'In broad biblical perspective, few concepts are more basic to the identity of God's people than being chosen by God.'[59] The qualification of πίστις by ἐκλεκτῶν indicates that this anarthrous usage refers to belief placed in Christ by specific people rather than the content of the Christian gospel.[60]

Paul is emphatic about who will receive faith: it is those chosen (ἐκλεκτός - *eklektos*) by God: the elect (cf. 2 Tim. 1:8-9; 2:10; Rom. 8:33; Col. 3:12; John 15:16). 'The phrase (ἐκλεκτός θεοῦ - *eklektos Theou*) is never used in the NT to refer to people who have not yet responded to God's call.'[61] We cannot dilute the doctrine of predestination when confronted with such a conclusive statement. Everything is under God's sovereign control, hence the 'slavish' nature of Paul's position before God and God's sovereign will as to those who are chosen (elected) by him. 'Paul, an apostle for the purpose of helping God's elect people to believe.'[62]

> Throughout his writings, Paul insists that believers are those chosen by God apart from any merit of their own. Ephesians 1:4 says that God 'chose us in [Christ] before the foundation of the world.' Paul adds, 'In love he pre-

---

[59] R. W. Yarbrough, *The Letters to Timothy and Titus*. PNTC (Grand Rapids: Eerdmans, 2018), 468.

[60] Perkins, *The Pastoral Letters*, 243.

[61] Greenlee, *Titus and Philemon*, 14.

[62] Greenlee, *Titus and Philemon*, 14.

destined us for adoption to himself as sons through Jesus Christ' (Eph. 1:5). There are some who deny what Reformed scholars teach as *unconditional election*, suggesting instead that God chose us according to some merit that we first possess or condition that we have fulfilled. Usually, such teachers assert that God chose us only after he had foreseen our faith. But Paul teaches that we were chosen not *because of* faith but *to* faith. Predestination is by sovereign grace alone, 'according to the purpose of His will, to the praise of His glorious grace' (vv 5-6). John Calvin comments that in speaking of 'God's elect', Paul 'points out that faith does not begin with us. It is because God has chosen us, because of His immutable election and because of the unmerited goodness which He showed in adopting us as His children, that He gave us to Jesus Christ.'[63] John Calvin, *Sermons on Titus*, trans. Robert White (Edinburgh: Banner of Truth, 2015), 14.

καὶ ἐπίγνωσιν ἀληθείας τῆς κατ' εὐσέβειαν
and the knowledge of the truth that is consistent with godliness

'The use of 'κατὰ πίστιν ... κατ' ἐπίγνωσιν' (*kata pistin ... kai epignōsin*) in this verse has the intention of linking faith with knowledge. Faith and knowledge define two of the chief ends the apostolic worker has before him.'[64] 'Truth' (ἀλήθεία – *alētheia*) is a critical issue in Paul's theology. In *Titus* Paul regularly uses 'the truth' to refer to the gospel. The truth is 'in Jesus' (Eph. 4:21; John 17:17) and Paul spoke the word of truth in his preaching (Rom. 9:1). Paul's mission was not only to preach faith in Christ but also to ensure that every Christian had a knowledge of the truth, which is 'in accordance with godliness' (cf. 1

[63] Doriani & Phillips, *2 Timothy and Titus*, 129-30. See also MacArthur, *1-2 Timothy and Titus*, 4.

[64] Kelly, *A Commentary on the Pastoral Epistles*, 226.

Tim. 6:3).[65] 'God's servants are not intended to be ignorant in the field of truth, nor is their knowledge to be out of keeping with their religious profession.'[66] For this reason, Paul writes about the knowledge (ἐπίγνωσις – *epignōsis*) of the truth. It is knowledge that comes through faith. This word implies a thorough understanding of what is being taught. It is more than intellectual comprehension; rather, it is an appetite to know more about Christ and God (cf. 2 Tim. 3:7). 'Both truth and falsehood can be discerned by what they produce. God's **truth** produces **godliness**. The transformation wrought through saving faith is visibly manifest in holy conduct.'[67]

The combination of faith, and practice consistent with that faith, has always been required of the committed Christian. Bernard notes that 'it is only in a life of godliness (see on 1 Tim. 2:2 for εὐσέβεια) that the 'knowledge of the truth' can be fully learnt (see on 1 Tim. 4:3).'[68] Paul's emphasis on 'knowledge' reflects his continual emphasis that renewal of the mind is the first step in commencing the Christian life. In Romans 12:2 he insists that transformation from the present age to God's kingdom comes 'by the renewing of your mind' so that 'you may prove what the will of God is, that which is good and acceptable and perfect': faith followed by action.

Paul's and Titus' preaching was to be in accord with godliness. 'Godliness is the manifestation of the Spirit's work of sanctification.'[69] It is the moral response to faith, knowledge and truth. The practice of God's truth produces godliness. *Titus* warns us against false teaching, which produces ungodliness in its wake.

---

65 M. Zerwick and M. Grosvenor, *An Analysis of the Greek New Testament*. vol. 2 (Rome: Biblical Institute Press, 1979), 647.

66 D. Guthrie, *The Pastoral Epistles*. TNTC (Leicester: IVP, 1957), 182.

67 MacArthur, *1-2 Timothy and Titus*, 8 (original emphasis).

68 Bernard, *The Pastoral Epistles*, 155.

69 MacArthur, *1-2 Timothy and Titus*, 7.

> There is an intimate connection between truth and godliness. A vital possession of truth is inconsistent with irreverence. ... Real truth never deviates from the path of piety. A profession of the truth which allows an individual to live in ungodliness is a spurious profession.[70]

Jesus warned in Matthew 7:15-17:

> 15 'Beware of the false prophets, who come to you in sheep's clothing, but inwardly are ravenous wolves.
> 16 You will know them by their fruits. Grapes are not gathered from thorn bushes nor figs from thistles, are they?
> 17 So every good tree bears good fruit, but the bad tree bears bad fruit.'
> NASB

1:2 in Detail

ἐπ' ἐλπίδι ζωῆς αἰωνίου
(based) on the hope of eternal life

Paul's apostleship is not for the present, momentary benefit of his hearers. It is supposed to have long-term benefits. Paul serves as a slave and apostle so that their knowledge of Christ is based on the hope (ἐλπίς – *elpis*) of eternal life. 'As a Jew, and drawing from the Old Testament, Paul carried the conviction that beyond this world lay another, already inhabited and prepared by God.'[71] 'This hope is an earnest yearning, confident expectation and patient waiting for "life everlasting", salvation in its fullest development (cf. John 17:24; Rom. 8:25).'[72] The first Greek word

---

70 D. E. Hiebert, *Titus and Philemon* (Chicago: Moody Publishers, 1957), 21.

71 Yarbrough, *The Letters to Timothy and Titus*, 469.

72 Köstenberger, *Commentary on 1-2 Timothy and Titus*, 340-41; see esp. fn. 189 on 'hope'.

ἐπ' (abbreviated form of ἐπί (*epi*)) has a wide variety of meanings in the NT determined by its context.

> The NIV sees it (probably correctly) as modifying faith and knowledge (hence the repetition of these words in the translation). But rather than **faith and knowledge** resting on the **hope of eternal life**, as their eschatological basis (cf. BAGD), this phrase is better understood as sequential to them – as their ultimate goal.[73]

Greenlee notes that 'although Paul's apostleship is not governed by their faith, it is in harmony with it.'[74] From a biblical perspective,

> To hope means to look forward expectantly for God's future activity. The ground of hope is God's past activity in Jesus Christ, who points the way to God's purposes for His creation. ... But a Christian's hope is not utopian. He expects progress but not the perfection which will only come by God's own act at the final coming of Christ. He can cope with human failure without despair, because he trusts 'the God of hope' (Rom. 15:13) whose kingdom is surely coming.[75]

This hope is for *eternal* life (αἰώνιος ζωή - *aiōnios zōē*), which is a far deeper concept than everlasting life. Eternal life in a believer commences at the time of conversion: it is a present reality, yet it also comprises everlastingness. It is a *superior* life derived from a relationship with Christ and 'guarantees a continuity of relationship to Christ even through death.'[76] The hope of eternal life gives strength and endurance to those believers who experience suffering or persecution for Christ's sake.

---

[73] Fee, *1 & 2 Timothy, Titus*, 129 (original emphasis).

[74] Greenlee, *Titus and Philemon*, 14.

[75] S. H. Travis, *Hope* in S. B. Ferguson and D. Wright (eds), *New Dictionary of Theology* (Leicester: Inter-Varsity Press, 1988), 321-22.

[76] S. H. Travis, *Eschatology* in *New Dictionary of Theology*, 230.

> The future God promises is more powerful in this fallen world than the seemingly intractable evil and setbacks than can easily darken church leaders' vision, skew their judgment, and extinguish their hope.[77]

ἣν ἐπηγγείλατο ὁ ἀψευδὴς θεὸς πρὸ χρόνων αἰωνίων which God, who cannot lie, promised long ages ago

'This is the only place in the Pauline epistles in which the verb ἐπηγγείλατο (*epēngeilato*) means "promise" rather than "make a claim" as in 1 Tim. 2:10; 6:21.'[78] It seems somewhat redundant to suggest that the God, whose attributes include purity, truth and holiness, would not lie (ἀψευδὴς – *apseudēs*) but Paul nevertheless confirms it (cf. Num. 23:19; 1 Sam. 15:29). This word implies 'knowing no falsehood'.[79] Paul knows this but adds to the solidity of this hope by emphasising its reliable source (cf. Rom. 3:4).

> In 1.2 God is described as αψευδής. While the idea of God's truthfulness and dependability is pervasive in the biblical literature,[45] the term αψευδής is a biblical *hapax*. Against the background of endemically deceitful Crete the introduction of ὁ αψευδὴς θεός (1.2) could be heard as a contrast with lying humans, whether the Cretans in general (1.12) or specifically the envisaged opponents (1.14),[46] but there may also be a polemical contrast with the Cretans' god.[47] Another encounter between Christian missionaries and worshippers of Zeus is illustrated in the account in the book of Acts of the experience of Barnabas and Paul in Lystra (Acts 14.8-18). In the speech attributed to the missionaries in Acts 14.15-17, C. Breytenbach finds an 'Anti-Zeus-Tendenz', presenting the 'living God' in terms that directly challenge claims made on Zeus's behalf in Asia Minor in the first century CE. In a missionary approach to Crete, jealous of its association with Zeus, the declaration

[77] Yarbrough, *The Letters to Timothy and Titus*, 470.
[78] Perkins, *The Pastoral Letters*, 245.
[79] Zerwick & Grosvenor, *Analysis of the Greek New Testament*, vol. 2, 647.

of ὁ αψευδὴς θεός, the God who does not lie, would be a plausible strategy: in this instance not claiming for God activities and qualities for which Zeus had been given credit, but suggesting a contrast between a deceitful and capricious pagan deity and the truthful and dependable God of Christian missionary proclamation.[80]

[45] In the OT Balaam confesses, 'God is not a human being, that he should lie' (Num. 23.19) and Ps. 89.35 (LXX 88.36) has God declare, 'Once and for all I have sworn in my holiness; I will not lie to David!' (εἰ τῷ Δαυίδ ψεύσομαι). In the NT, Heb. 6.18 cites God's promise and oath as two things in which 'it is impossible that God would prove false' (αδύνατον ψεὺσασθαι [τον] θεὸν). In both Hebrews and *Titus* the considerations that buttressed OT faith in God's promises now support a faith that interprets them in Christian terms (Tit. 3.6; Heb. 6:11-12, 17).

[46] As suggested by Marshall, *Pastoral Epistles*, 126. Faber ('*Evil Beasts, Lazy Gluttons* 135-45) develops the argument that in citing Callimachus's accusation the author of *Titus* is implying that just as Cretans held heterodox views in relation to traditional beliefs about Zeus, now 'the false teachers hold theological convictions that are opposed to the truth' (138).

[47] R. M. Kidd refers to traditions of Zeus's deception, concluding, 'And that Titus' biblically unique reference to the Christian God as being "unlying" stands in self-conscious contradistinction to a chief deity whom Titus' Paul would consider to be an immoral liar I consider to be altogether likely' ('Titus as Apologia: Grace for Liars, Beasts, and Bellies', *Horizons in Biblical Theology* 21 [1999] 185-209 [198]). Cf. P. H. Towner's suggestion that the reference to a God who does not lie 'could well lampoon the character of the Zeus of Cretan tales, who in fact did lie to have sexual relations with a human woman' (*The Letters to Timothy and Titus* [NICNT; Grand Rapids: Eerdmans, 2006], 670).

80 See G. M. Weiland, 'Roman Crete and the Letter to Titus', *NTS* vol. 55, no. 3 2009, 346-47.

This issue is specifically discussed by Peter Jensen in terms of Christian doctrine. 'His law is an expression of his character, and his character does not vary. Were he to announce that telling lies was now permitted, for example, it would be tantamount to lying.'[81] Hebrews 6:18 confirms that 'it is impossible for God to lie'.

This hope of eternal life was promised (ἐπαγγέλλομαι – *epangellomai*) by God Himself 'before times eternal' (πρὸ χρόνων αἰωνίων – *pro chronōn aiōniōn*). Paul uses a different form of the verb to say the same thing in Romans 4:21. There the verb προεπαγγέλλω (*proepangellō*) contains the understanding of a promise made beforehand. *In this verse we see both aspects of eternity.* The aorist tense confirms the certainty that the promise was pre-determined and certain of fulfillment. Earlier, *aiōnios* referred to eternity in the context of everlastingness. Here its use implies no beginning.

> This is very striking. How can a promise be made before the world began? To whom could it be made? The Scripture here speaks of a promise made by the Father to the Son or to the Holy Spirit because, after all, at this particular point of sequence there was no one else to make the promise to.
>
> Finally, the same point is made in 2 Timothy 1:9, where we read about God, 'who hath saved us, and called us with an holy calling, not according to our works, but according to his own purpose and grace, which was given us in Christ Jesus before the world began.'
>
> We are faced, therefore with a very interesting question: When did history begin? If one is thinking with the modern concept of the space-time continuum, then it is quite obvious that time and history did not exist before 'in the beginning.' But if we are thinking of history in contrast

[81] P. F. Jensen, *The Life of Faith: An Introduction to Christian Doctrine* (Sydney: Matthias Media, 2022), 100.

> to an eternal, philosophic other or in contrast to a static eternal, then history began before Genesis 1:1.[82]
>
> God is beyond time as we understand it.
>
> If God perceives past, present and future with a perfect understanding, it is easy to think of him as 'timeless', or better, 'eternal' - that is, as existing without history or future but in identical relation with all that has been, is, and will be (indeed, in identical relation with all possible events past and future as well). This being so, most Christian thinkers seem to have adopted such a position and wish to argue that the universe was created with time, there being no possibility of time as such until some part of creation came into being: 'Thus there can be no doubt that the world was not created *in* time but *with* time.'*.[83]
> *Augustine, *City of God*, XI.6.

The reality of eternal life is that it has always existed but can only be received by believers (John 3:15-16), who then enjoy God's eternity forever.

1:3 in Detail

ἐφανέρωσεν δὲ καιροῖς ἰδίοις τὸν λόγον αὐτοῦ
but at the proper time made known His word,

The NASB addition of '*even*' in this phrase is unnecessary. It is not implied by the Greek text. Although promised from eternity, there had to be a time when eternal life was realised for humanity. Paul writes that it was 'revealed' (ἐφανέρωσεν – *ephanerōsen*) 'at the proper time' (καιρος ἴδίος – *kairos idios*) (cf. 1 Tim. 2:6; 6:15).[84] 'The word *kairos* denotes

---

82 F. A. Schaeffer, *Genesis in Space and Time*, in F. A. Schaeffer, *The Complete Works of Francis A. Schaeffer: A Christian Worldview*. second ed., 5 vols. (Wheaton, IL: Crossway, 1983), vol. 2, 9.

83 Jensen, *Life of Faith*, 96.

84 'The plural form applies to a single event in 1 Tim. 6:15 (see also 1 Tim. 2:6 where the same phrase occurs), and it should probably be understood here in the same fashion.' Perkins, *The Pastoral Letters*, 245.

a suitable opportunity as compared with *chronos* used for duration or succession of time.'[85] The NT use of this Greek verb implies something that 'appeared', was 'made visible', and 'disclosed' at a particular time.[86] Wallace suggests that the meaning of 'the proper time' is 'something like "just at the right moment"'.[87] 'Paul reminds Titus of the epochal, cosmic, and temporal "cross"-road at which he and the Cretan churches stand.'[88] Although Paul's reference here is the manifestation of God's word through his preaching, we should not forget that the 'proper time' can also be understood as the time set by the foreknowledge of God in the birth of Jesus, who was both the Word of God as well as the one who would speak the words of God (cf. 1 John 1:2). His entry into this world as a person occurred at the 'proper' time of which the prophets foretold repeatedly in the OT (cf. Is. 42:1-4). 'God promised eternal life before eternal times, but he manifested his word at the proper time.'[89] As far as Jews and Gentiles are concerned (in Paul's evangelistic ministry), the proper time for them is hearing the preaching of the gospel of Christ.

> But as in 1 Corinthians 2:7–10 (cf. 2 Tim. 1:9; Eph. 1:4), Paul's point is that what believers are now experiencing belongs to the eternal counsels of God and has been hidden in God until revealed by the Spirit in the present Age through the work of Christ (cf. Rom. 16:25-26; Col. 1:25–26).[90]

---

85 Guthrie, *The Pastoral Epistles*, 182.

86 *The Strongest NASB Exhaustive Concordance*, Greek Dictionary (Grand Rapids: Zondervan, 2000), 1575.

87 D. B. Wallace, *Greek Grammar Beyond the Basics* (Grand Rapids: Zondervan, 1996), 157. See Yarbrough, *The Letters to Timothy and Titus*, 472, Table 25 regarding Paul's use of *kairos*.

88 Yarbrough, *The Letters to Timothy and Titus*, 472.

89 Greenlee, *Titus and Philemon*, 18.

90 Fee, *1 & 2 Timothy, Titus*, 129.

ἐν κηρύγματι ὃ ἐπιστεύθην ἐγὼ κατ᾽ ἐπιταγὴν τοῦ σωτῆρος ἡμῶν θεοῦ,
in the preaching with which I was entrusted according to the commandment of God our Saviour,

In human terms, the word of God is manifested through the preaching (κήρυγμα - *kērugma*) of the gospel, as Titus is well aware from his long association with Paul, who is continuing the preaching of the gospel begun by Christ (cf. 1 Tim. 1:11).[91] This is an ongoing process, often overlooked by modern commentators. Preaching the gospel today continues this tradition first exampled by Paul's preaching of the gospel. The *word* was made known because *eternal life* was still in the future for believers. Again, Paul returns to the theme of his personal commissioning for this task by 'the commandment of God our Saviour' (τοῦ σωτῆρος ἡμῶν θεοῦ – *tou sōtēros hēmōn Theou*). The word 'Saviour' is used in *Titus* as many times (six) as it is used in all the other Pauline letters put together. This word clearly has some resonance with the Cretans.

In light of the frequent use of the term 'Saviour' in the letter to Titus (1:3, 4; 2:10, 13; 3:4, 6; cf. 1 Tim. 1:1; 2 Tim. 1:10), it's noteworthy that an inscription was found at the sanctuary of Asclepius at Lebena near Gortyn, reading, 'Diodorus dedicated to you, Saviour, two dreams in return for twofold eyes, light being restored' (2nd century AD?). Another similar Greek inscription, addressed to Zeus and attributed to a Corinthian named Plotius, was found at Knossos. This evidence for the use of 'Saviour' pertaining to Greek deities provides a crucial backdrop for Paul's references to God and Jesus as 'Saviour,' designating them as the true provider and exclusive mediator of salvation, respectively. [92]

---

[91] See Yarbrough, *The Letters to Timothy and Titus*, 473.

[92] A. J. Köstenberger, *1-2 Timothy & Titus*. Biblical Theology for Christian Proclamation (Nashville: B&H, 2017), 298.

Note Paul's insertion of 'I' (ἐγὼ - *egō*) to emphasise his specific, personal appointment by God, rather than some task of his own initiative. Throughout his ministry, Paul was at pains to emphasise his divine election to this task of preaching to the *Gentiles* (Gal. 1:15): an important fact in the context of this letter to Titus, who was living among the Gentiles (and Jews) of Crete.

> Paul's gospel proclamation, which was grounded in a special commissioning by the risen Christ (Acts 9:15-16), took place by the command (ἐπιταγή, [Tit.] 2:15; see on 1 Tim. 1:1) of 'God our Saviour' (see on 1 Tim. 1:1). ***Paul consistently rooted his preaching in divine revelation rather than viewing it merely as a human message.*** The gospel originated with God, not Paul. By identifying God, and later Jesus, as Saviour, Paul establishes a theocentric, Christocentric, and soteriological framework for the entire letter (the pattern recurs in 2:10, 13, and 3:4, 6), where Jesus is presented as both God in His own right (2:13) and the fulfillment of God's saving promises.[93]

'Saviour' is a description of God or Christ used by Paul in the latter part of his life. He hardly ever uses 'Saviour' in his earlier letters (cf. Eph. 5:23; Phlp. 3:30) but uses the word in 1 Timothy, 2 Timothy and *Titus* to refer to both God (1 Tim. 1:1; 2:3; 4:10; Tit. 1:3; 2:10; 2:13) and Christ (2 Tim. 1:10; Tit. 1:4; 3:6) as Saviour. There can be no doubt by this usage that Paul reinforces the divinity of Christ and His oneness with the Father. Pauline theology is Trinitarian.

> Ultimately what Paul has done in this introduction is to place his own apostolate at the centre of God's story: his authority and message are essential to it and derive their meaning from it. Thus, Paul is authenticating the ministry

---

93 Köstenberger, *1-2 Timothy & Titus*, 309 (emphasis added). This issue is particularly relevant to 1:14. See also Yarbrough, *The Letters to Timothy and Titus*, 474.

of his coworker Titus by establishing his own authority to instruct Titus.[94]

1:4 in Detail

τίτῳ γνησίῳ τέκνῳ κατὰ κοινὴν πίστιν
To Titus, my true child in a common faith:

Paul's letter is addressed to Titus, one of his most trusted and longstanding companions (see Introduction). The generosity and warm-heartedness evident in Paul's description of Titus shows the depth of relationship between the two men. Paul had 'begotten' innumerable children of God (John 1:12) through his preaching (1 Cor. 4:15) as well as acting as a father to young (in faith) Christians (1 Thess. 2:11) but we only see his close personal affection for a few colleagues in his letters. It is only of Timothy (1 Tim. 1:2) and Titus that the apostle sees fit to apply the designation 'my true child' (γνήσιος τέκνον - *gnēsios teknon*).[95] In 1:2 Paul speaks of truth (and lies) regarding factual words and circumstances. However, his description of Titus as a 'true' son does not fall into this category. Here, 'true' (*gnēsios*) indicates genuineness: 'it refers to Titus' authenticity - he is genuine in his conviction and service; as a disciple and a coworker, he is the real thing'.[96] Paul's knows that he can completely rely on Titus' faithfulness to implement his instructions in this letter. It should also be noted that the nature of Paul's greeting would have reassured Titus of Paul's full confidence in him.[97]

---

94 P. H. Towner. *The Letters to Timothy and Titus*, 664.

95 Paul does apply 'child' in his description of Onesimus (Phlm. 10).

96 Yarbrough, *The Letters to Timothy and Titus*, 474.

97 I. H. Marshall with P. H. Towner, *The Pastoral Epistles*. ICC (Edinburgh: T. & T. Clark, 1999), 133.

> Titus was the direct legate, envoy, or ambassador of the apostle, sent to Crete to strengthen the churches for the purpose of effective evangelism in that pagan culture. Anyone, therefore, who attacked the authority and teaching of Titus would be attacking the divinely delegated authority and teaching of Paul himself.[98]

The 'sonship' of Titus (and Timothy) with respect to Paul relates to his shared belief with Paul in the power of the gospel and faith in Jesus Christ. Titus and Paul share a 'common faith' (κοινὴ πίστις - *koinē pistis*).[99] Köestenberger suggests that the reference to their 'common faith' 'may be designed to convey unity between Paul as a Jew and Titus as a Gentile.'[100] Mounce describes it as 'the usual Pauline sense of a believing response that binds Paul the Jew and Titus the Gentile together, a significant point in light of the Jewish nature of the heresy being taught in Crete.'[101] There is much debate as to the meaning and content of this simple term 'the faith'. Two types of faith should be considered here. The first is *fides quae creditur,* which is an objective, established body of doctrine or belief that can be documented and/or assented to.[102] The second is *fides qua creditur,* which is a believer's own acknowledgement of faith in God. To which does Paul refer? It is the first in this instance. In the NT, Paul uses several terms when discussing what Christians should believe, particularly

---

98 MacArthur, *1-2 Timothy and Titus*, 2.

99 This issue is discussed at greater length concerning Jude 3 in Manuell, *Letter of Jude*, 93-95. See Yarbrough, *Letters to Timothy and Titus*, 474-5. This is the only occurrence of κοινὴ in the pastoral epistles.

100 Köstenberger, *1-2 Timothy & Titus*, 309. See Fee, *1 & 2 Timothy, Titus*, 170.

101 Mounce, *Pastoral Epistles*, 382.

102 Examples are the Apostles' Creed and the Nicene Creed.

in circumstances where they are subject to challenge or where contrary beliefs are asserted.[103]

These beliefs were delivered from God the Father through the Holy Spirit (John 15:26–7), just as the Mosaic Law had its divine origin at Mount Sinai (Ex. 34:27). These beliefs were entrusted to the apostles in the first century for all time. 'The faith' is therefore entrusted from one generation to another *without alteration*. The use in Jude 3 of ἅπαξ (*hapax* - once for all) should be understood in the light of Hebrews 9:26–28 and 1 Peter 3:18. The meaning there is 'something done uniquely, only once, once for all'.[104] It is not just that God has provided insight into His purposes on one occasion, and this might change over time. On the contrary, these basic tenets of the faith were intended to stand forever. It is this firm foundation that Jude encouraged his readers to defend (Matt. 16:18; Jude 3). The later-dated books of the NT stress this need to adhere to tradition more strongly than earlier ones.[105] As pure doctrine was being compromised by errorists (1:9), it became increasingly urgent for Paul to insist that 'the faith' be maintained (cf. Jude 3).

The extent to which 'the faith' (the gospel) might be subject to alteration is well explained by I. H. Marshall:

> Two points, however, must be noted. On the one hand, the writer is not saying anything handed down from the past is true and reliable simply because of its antiquity. He regards the teaching given at the beginning as issuing from the Lord through the apostles and hence bearing the

---

[103] It should be noted that, other than in Paul's letters, there are no written formulae of Christian doctrine at this early stage of Christianity. Formal creeds were only adopted centuries later.

[104] T. Friberg, B. Friberg and N. F. Miller, *Analytical Lexicon of the Greek New Testament* (Grand Rapids: Baker Books, 2000), 61. See G. L. Green, *Jude and 2 Peter*, 56-57 concerning the importance in the first century of the handing down of tradition.

[105] In reality, this faith should be common to all Christians for all time. See Greenlee, *Titus and Philemon*, 20.

> stamp of divine revelation; it is 'the word of Christ' which is to 'dwell in you richly' (Col. 2:21-22). On the other hand, while the writer is clearly opposed to new fashions and innovations in doctrine which are false, he would no doubt allow that what has been handed down as 'truth unchanged, unchanging' may need to be re-expressed in fresh ways if it is to make the same impact on modern readers as it made on its first readers. The art of translation is to reproduce by means of the receptor language the same impression on the readers in its original language. What is true of different languages is also true of presenting the gospel to people in different ages and cultures.[106]

There has been a good deal of debate as to the nature and, particularly, the content of this faith that had to be protected. Some commentators regard this 'faith' as a term comparable to the beliefs that Paul espoused when he used the term 'gospel' (cf. Phlp. 1:27). Others have enlarged its meaning to encompass a set body of doctrine that might have even been reduced to written form. While this latter suggestion is going too far at the time *Titus* was written, it is the case that Paul's letters do contain what we might call doctrinal propositions (e.g., 1 Cor. 15:1–8, 11.)

When Paul wrote his letters, it is difficult to assert that, apart from some fundamental statements, he would have regarded 'the faith' as a rigid statement of belief. Paul refers to the same concept in the same context as *Jude*, using the same word (*pistis*) in Colossians 2:7: 'now being built up in Him and established in your faith, *just as you were instructed*' (my emphasis). It was not until AD 325 that the Nicene Creed was adopted as a definitive statement of Christian belief. Nevertheless, Paul insists that 'the faith' (however defined) is an unchanging truth (1 Cor. 16:13; Gal. 3:23, 25; 6:10; Phlp. 1:25; Col. 1:23), as

[106] I. H. Marshall, *The Epistles of John* (Grand Rapids: Eerdmans, 1978), 160.

would the author of Hebrews (3:6, 14; 4:14; 10:23). Because there is no indication in *Titus* of a formal church structure or organisation, it is reasonable to assume that Titus' 'faith' is more equivalent to Paul's 'gospel' than to the later formulations of a more established church. But this conclusion should not rule out the possibility that Titus' 'faith' contained elements of both *fides qua creditur* and *fides quae creditur,* even if more of the latter: 'only earnest believers contend for what they believe.'[107]

χάρις καὶ εἰρήνη ἀπὸ θεοῦ πατρὸς καὶ χριστοῦ ἰησοῦ τοῦ σωτῆρος ἡμῶν.
Grace and peace from God the Father and Christ Jesus our Saviour.

Grace and peace emanate from the one true God; therefore, it is logical that they are given by the Father and His Son. This is the same greeting as in Romans 1:7.

God is rich in *mercy* (Eph. 2:4). Without God's mercy, it would be impossible for humanity to survive His wrath. The first mention of mercy (Hebrew: *hesed*) in the Bible is God's mercy, which occurs in Genesis 19:19, with the story of Lot and his family being saved from the destruction of Sodom. Mercy is not a human construct. Mercy is a divine prerogative and, by grace, God has imbued it in the human conscience. It is appropriate that God is the first-mentioned giver of mercy in the story of redemption. It is from His mercy towards helpless sinners that God set in plan the redemption of humanity through Christ before the foundation of the world (Eph. 1:4).[108] Mercy is closely linked to rescue (Gen. 19:19) and salvation. When Mary learns of her pregnancy, she exclaims that 'He [God] has given *help* to Israel His servant, in remembrance of

107 R. C. H. Lenski, *The Interpretation of the Epistles of St Peter, St John and St Jude*. (Minneapolis: Augsburg Publishing House, 1966), 610.

108 See L. Berkhof, *Systematic Theology* (Edinburgh: Banner of Truth, 1976), 72.

His *mercy*' (Luke 1:54, emphasis added). When John the Baptist is born, his father, Zecharias, pronounces that his son will be a prophet who will give Israel 'the *knowledge of salvation* by the forgiveness of their sins, *because of the tender mercy of our God*' (Luke 1:77-78, emphasis added).

Paul would have been quite familiar with *hesed* from his reading of the OT Scriptures in Hebrew. It is a concept of deep significance in Judaism, for *it is probably the closest OT term for the NT term 'grace'* (Χάρις - *charis*).[109] *Hesed* is closely associated with the Abrahamic covenant (Genesis 12) and Dumbrell notes importantly that *hesed*

> does not arise from a sense of obligation, i.e. merely from a legally binding commitment, but from a sense of personal loyalty which the relationship involves. The point has been made that the word *hesed* is not applicable to the establishment of a relationship, but *reflects rather fidelity and loyalty to an existing relationship*. The aim of the *hesed* exhibited is to preserve the tenor of the relationship which already exists.'[110]

Paul begins his greeting with 'grace' because that is the foundation on which Titus' (and our) relationship with God is based: the divine initiative to extend mercy and blessing to Abraham, even before he recognised its existence, is grace.

From grace emanates *peace* (εἰρήνη — *eirēnē*). This can be peace in a general sense, but it is much more likely to be the peace of God the Father and the Lord Jesus Christ

---

[109] The parallel meaning of *hesed* and *charis* is not universally accepted by commentators.

[110] W. J. Dumbrell, *Covenant and Creation: An Old Testament Covenantal Theology* (Homebush West, NSW: Lancer Books, 1984), 106 (emphasis added); see also 19, 194. See Dumbrell for a comprehensive analysis of the continuity of God's covenant with humanity (and the created order) from creation to eternity. See also F. I. Andersen, 'Yahweh, the Kind and Sensitive God' in *God Who Is Rich in Mercy: Essays Presented to Dr D. B. Knox*. eds P. T. O'Brien and D. G. Peterson (Homebush West, NSW: Lancer Books, 1986), 41-44.

(cf. Phlp. 1:2; 1 Thess. 1:1; 1 Tim. 1:2). The primary Jewish greeting is *shalom* (peace) and it seems obvious that Paul would wish this for his close associate. Note that these references are greetings at the start of a letter. For Jews like Paul, this automatically recalls the concept of peace (favour, safety, welfare) conveyed by *shalom* (Gen. 15:15). Having accepted God's gifts of mercy and grace through the atoning sacrifice (propitiation) of Christ, Paul declares that Christians can then enjoy peace with God. The divine/human relationship has been restored through Christ. This also means that the individual's peace with God can then flow outwards to fellow believers and others. In this way, the peace of God is multiplied towards these believers as the church grows.[111]

In contrast to the previous verse, Paul nominates Christ Jesus as Saviour. Clearly, the Father and the Son form a unity in Paul's theology. 'The interchanging of this title [Saviour] between God and Christ Jesus (cf. 3:4, 6) reflects the high Christology found in Paul from the beginning.'[112]

The Situation in Crete

1:5 *For this reason I left you in Crete, that you would set in order what remains and appoint elders in every city as I directed you.*
NASB

---

111 Yarbrough, *Letters to Timothy and Titus*, 475, n 39 notes: 'Some manuscripts (including A C2 K L 81, the Textus Receptus, and others) insert "mercy" (*eleos*) after "grace". Metzger, *Textual Commentary* (1984), 584, notes that Paul definitely writes "grace, mercy, and peace" in 1 Tim. 1:2; 2 Tim. 1:2. On this basis scribes may have added "mercy" to Titus 1:4. But "mercy" could have been present originally, with some early scribes opting for the familiar Pauline "grace and peace".' It is noteworthy that Jude 2 uses 'mercy and peace and love.'

112 Fee, *1 & 2 Timothy, Titus*, 130.

Notwithstanding the order of Paul's guidance in *Titus*, appointing elders seems to be the initial task, then setting things in order (whatever they were). Then the appointed elders could assist Titus in his work of proclamation.

> Paul's instructions reflect his intimate knowledge of the local situation on Crete, but also speak generally for all who engage in church-planting work. Indeed, the themes in Titus speak to any church that desires to be sound and growing. We may summarize Paul's concerns as addressing the need for godly leadership (Tit. 1:5–16), sound doctrinal teaching (2:1–15), and holy living (3:1–15). These same ingredients are essential for more established churches as well as young ones.
>
> It is significant for the message of this letter to Titus that, while Paul left his protégé in Crete to set the church in order (Tit. 1:5), the letter does not address church organization as such. Instead, it brims with the message of God's grace as it is practically applied.[113]

1:5 in Detail

5 τούτου χάριν ἀπέλιπόν σε ἐν κρήτῃ, ἵνα τὰ λείποντα ἐπιδιορθώσῃ
For this reason I deployed[114] you in Crete, that you might set right what remains to be done[115]

Titus has remained in Crete to fulfil specific instructions from Paul. Although Titus must appoint elders, we are left to guess what other tasks need to be completed. 'But for various reasons, some of which will emerge below, until the pastoral pool could be enlarged, enhanced, or

[113] Doriani & Phillips, *2 Timothy and Titus*, 126.

[114] See Perkins, *The Pastoral Letters*, 247.

[115] See Zerwick and Grosvenor, *Analysis of the Greek New Testament*, vol. 2, 647 for the translation of τὰ λείποντα ἐπιδιορθώσῃ.

both, Paul's command to "put in order" what was awry or lacking had only dim prospects of effective implementation.'[116] The text of the letter certainly points to some areas of order and discipline but they are fairly general in nature. The qualifications described by Paul in this letter are like, but not the same as, those described in 1 Timothy 3, reflecting the need to cater for the different needs of the churches in Crete and Corinth (for Timothy). Paul wished Titus to build on their foundational work (cf. 1 Cor. 3:6). The words τὰ λείποντα ἐπιδιορθώσῃ (*ta leiponta epidiorthōsē*) suggest that, when Paul left Crete, there was unfinished business to be completed in the churches (see 3:13).

> Not only is ἐπιδιορθόω used only here in the NT, but the term is also extremely uncommon in pre-Christian Greek writings. Intriguingly, the sole written instance is found in a second-century BC inscription from Hierapytna, a Cretan city, with reference to the activity of a regional local administrator. Perhaps Titus' role mirrors that of a Cretan official.[117]

Clearly, Titus is well aware of these things. Paul doesn't need to repeat them. Appointing elders was just one of many tasks to be done, but one of the first. Other tasks would be to oppose and eliminate false teaching (1:11) and instruct various groups of Cretan Christians how to behave publicly and privately (2:2-6). The appointed elders would undoubtedly assist Titus in undertaking this mission. Gundry helpfully interprets Paul's instructions.

> 'I left you behind in Crete' implies that Paul had been in Crete. 'That you might set straight the remaining matters' implies that he had done some work there but left before finishing it, and that the work consisted in setting

[116] Yarbrough, *Letters to Timothy and Titus*, 477.

[117] MacArthur, *1-2 Timothy and Titus*, 312. Perkins, *The Pastoral Letters*, 248 notes: 'This verb is a NT *hapax* that means to "set right or correct in addition (to what has already been corrected)".'

> straight some matters that were threatening, or indeed were corrupting, the churches located there. Titus had the job of appointing elders so that they might help in setting straight those matters, for by virtue of their status and appointment they'll have authority to help. 'City by city' implies the existence of a number of local churches on Crete. 'As I ordered you' indicates that before Paul left he told Titus to appoint elders. So Paul is reminding Titus of that order, and this reminder of the order evolves into a reminder of qualifications for eldership.[118]

However, given the later text in the letter (1:10-16), this was to be no easy task. Titus would need to use his tact and skill in personal relationships to distinguish those who would be worthy of his trust and confidence.[119]

καὶ καταστήσῃς κατὰ πόλιν πρεσβυτέρους, ὡς ἐγώ σοι διεταξάμην.
and appoint elders in each city, as I directed you.

Titus was to appoint leaders for the Christians on Crete. From the Greek for 'elder' (πρεσβυτέρος - *presbuteros*) comes the denomination known as Presbyterians, with its emphasis on eldership. They were to be 'appointed' (καθίστημι - *kathistēmi*) by Titus in every town where there was a Christian community (as in Acts 14:23). There is no sense of 'ordination'. No doubt, many towns did not have believing Christians in their midst before the arrival of Paul and Titus. Mounce argues that the Cretan churches were relatively young: 'the second indication of the church's age is that there is no discussion of the removal of bad elders (cf. 1 Tim. 5:19-25). Titus is instructed to appoint elders where there previously were none, suggesting a

---

[118] Gundry, *Commentary on First and Second Timothy, Titus*, 62.

[119] See Introduction concerning Paul's (subsequently confirmed) confidence in sending Titus to address the difficulties in the Corinthian church (2 Cor. 12:18).

young church.' [120] It will be these elders who will assist Titus in maintaining the truth of the gospel and correcting the disobedient and disputers discussed later in the letter.

Paul's direction (διατάσσω - *diatassō*) to Titus is a stern command, not a suggestion (cf. 1 Cor. 7:17; 9:14; 11:34; 16:1). This word means 'to give detailed instructions'.[121] Note the personal commitment required of both Paul and Titus by Paul's insertion of ἐγώ (*egō* – I) and σοι (*soi* - you). ἐγώ is also another statement about Paul's apostolic authority in this matter. The text ('elders in *each* city') implies that several elders were to be appointed to each church. There is no suggestion of hierarchy where one (or some) elders are to have authority over others. The position is that all the elders needed to act together.

> So even though 'as I directed you' comes at the end of the verse and might appear to be an afterthought, it was not a phrase apt to encourage complacency in Titus. It might rather connote urgency,[41] if not slight pique, as in the idiom, 'Like I good and well told you'.[122]
>
> [41] The possibly emphatic use (but, see Turner, *Grammar of New Testament Greek*, 37) and position of the pronouns *egō* and *soi* in front of the verb 'directed' should also not be overlooked.

Qualifications for Church Leaders

1:6 *An elder must be blameless, faithful to his wife, a man whose children believe and are not open to the charge of being wild and disobedient.*

1:7 *Since an overseer manages God's household, he must be blameless – not overbearing, not quick-tempered, not*

[120] Mounce, *Pastoral Epistles*, 386.

[121] Perkins, *The Pastoral Letters*, 248.

[122] Yarbrough, *Letters to Timothy and Titus*, 477. See Mounce, *Pastoral Epistles*, 387.

given to drunkenness, not violent, not pursuing dishonest gain.

1:8 *Rather, he must be hospitable, one who loves what is good, who is self-controlled, upright, holy and disciplined.*

1:9 *He must hold firmly to the trustworthy message as it has been taught, so that he can encourage others by sound doctrine and refute those who oppose it.*

NASB

Here we have the beginning of the essence of Paul's letter, which is relevant to all the churches in Crete with specific instructions for various groups: continually do good works to both Christians and society at large with exemplary behaviour and be aware of the impression you give to those outside the church. How relevant are these instructions to churches and Christians today!

Paul had visited Crete with Titus (we know not when) and 'left' (ἀπέλιπόν – *apelipon*) (but not abandoned) his companion to complete some specific tasks regarding the Christians on the island. The context suggests that Paul and Titus spent sufficient time on Crete for evangelism, which had produced some converts. However, these young (in faith) Christians had to be organised into an efficient body with leaders to be appointed from amongst themselves. This would not be possible unless Paul was confident that at least a few men had properly understood and committed themselves to the gospel. Clearly, there were some (presumably) administrative issues to be completed by Titus. We are given no hint as to the time which might be needed for such matters to be dealt with. In 1 Timothy 3:1-7 Paul provides a list of the qualities to be possessed by an elder. It is shorter than the list in *Titus* and comprises some different qualities. This may be explained because of a more developed church scene in Ephesus (to which Timothy was sent) than was the case in Crete, where more specific direction would need to be given to the new elders.

Paul's initial emphasis to Titus is not to combat false teaching (although that will have an important place in Titus' mission) but to organise the churches with strong leadership so that false teaching would have little opportunity to emerge. Nevertheless, v 10 indicates some initial problems in that regard. Therefore, like 1 Timothy 3, Paul describes the desired characteristics of those suitable for leadership (i.e. eldership), including undesirable qualities which were to be avoided.

1:6 in Detail

εἴ τίς ἐστιν ἀνέγκλητος,
If any man is blameless,

The letter now turns to the qualifications of these elders. It is noteworthy that, in the following instructions, there is the assumption that the home should be the first training ground for future Christians (and their leaders). Each of the requirements below needs direct application to the current leaders in our churches. Paul knew from long experience the type of men who would be suitable. The text provides no evidence that elders were appointed only from those who were older men (see 2:2). My emphasis is on *men* as church leaders. This is quite contrary to current thinking in most Christian denominations, which reject this notion under the false claims of 'discrimination' or 'equality'. My book, *Gender Wars in Christianity*, identified the creational distinctives between men and women and their roles in Christianity from a biblical perspective.[123]

> The world of our day has no fixed values and standards, and therefore what people conceive as their personal or society's happiness covers everything. We are not in that position. We have the inerrant Scripture. Looking to

[123] See G. Manuell, *Gender Wars in Christianity* (Brisbane: Connor Court, 2018).

> Christ for strength against tremendous pressure because our whole structure is against us at this point, we must reject the infiltration in theology and in life equally. We must both affirm the inerrancy of Scripture and then live under it in our personal lives and in society. None of us do this perfectly, but it must be the 'set' of our thinking and living. And when we fail, we must ask God's forgiveness.
>
> God's Word will never pass away, but looking back to the Old Testament and since the time of Christ, with tears we must say that because of lack of fortitude and faithfulness on the part of God's people, God's Word has many times been allowed to be bent, to conform to the surrounding, passing, changing culture of that moment rather than to stand as the inerrant Word of God judging the form of the world spirit and the surrounding culture of that moment. In the name of the Lord Jesus Christ, may your children and grandchildren not say that such can be said about us.[124]

Although the strength of Paul's insistence on these qualities is properly emphasised using 'must' in many translations: εἴ τὶς (*ei tis*) literally means 'if any man'. Paul's criterion for elders is effectively mandatory and 'must' captures this insistence. 'An elder must be blameless' (ἀνέγκλητος – *anenklētos*); i.e. 'a man of unimpeachable character' (NEB). Being human, elders cannot be without sin. Zerwick and Grosvenor translate this word as 'irreproachable'.[125] Although the word is used in 1 Timothy 3:10 regarding elders, and 1 Corinthians 1:8 (where 'blameless' is appropriate), the NIV translation 'free from accusation' in Colossians 1:22 seems to best describe the desired moral standing of these elders. This is possessing a moral character consistent with the gospel, not of the society around them. 'Here we have the first hint of what will become the dominant theme of the letter

---

[124] Schaeffer, *Great Evangelical Disaster*, 65.

[125] Zerwick and Grosvenor, *Analysis of the Greek New Testament*, vol. 2, 647. See Guthrie, *The Pastoral Epistles*, 184.

– good works with exemplary behaviour, with a concern for what outsiders think.'[126] There should be nothing in their *private or public* lives which could bring the gospel of Christ into disrepute.[127] Also, having been justified by God's grace, they stand 'blameless' in God's relationship to them.[128]

What can be done about this? The realistic answer is: Nothing! Nothing, unless the Holy Spirit moves ordinary men and women in the churches' pews to act decisively. Dismiss those elders whose behaviour is not 'free from accusation' and elect men who are 'blameless' so that churches may be administered by men of integrity. However, the matter of clergy involves considerably more complexity, which only increases in episcopal denominations (i.e. Roman Catholic, Anglican, Orthodox). It is possible, but unlikely, that individual congregations will be able to turn wayward clergy around. The relevant denomination would need to act. Gaining approval for sanctions against individual clergy has always been a complex business and the present climate of 'tolerance' amongst most denominations in the West suggests that official disciplinary action will never occur, except for egregious behaviour *condemned by society*, not the gospel. The other (very difficult) course of action is for Bible-believing Christians to no longer attend their current churches and find Christian fellowship elsewhere (within or outside their denomination).[129] This course of action

---

[126] Fee, *1 & 2 Timothy, Titus*, 133.

[127] This criterion stands in clear contrast to much modern thinking about our political leaders, where private indiscretions are not necessarily considered to be relevant to the performance of their public duties. A politician (and every person) either has integrity in the whole of their life or none at all. God holds us to account for every aspect of our lives.

[128] See Yarbrough, *Letters to Timothy and Titus*, 479-80 for a detailed analysis of what it means to be 'blameless'.

[129] This type of decision will have important ramifications for those who leave and for those Bible-believing Christians who remain.

should not be undertaken lightly but only after much prayer, consideration of the alternatives and discussion with like-minded believers. The gospel will only flourish under godly leadership.

μιᾶς γυναικὸς ἀνήρ,
a husband of one wife,

The NASB translation *'faithful to his wife'* does not do justice to Paul's requirement. The Greek reads literally 'of one wife a husband'. 'We may observe the same grammatical construction in 1 Timothy 5:9, where Paul commends worthy widows as "having been the wife of one husband." The point is not mere monogamy but, more pointedly, fidelity.'[130] Marital fidelity 'for most if not all human males, is a litmus test of their character in every other domain of their lives, at least as far as God is concerned, who sees the heart.'[131] Titus needed to deal with both Jews and Gentiles on Crete. The Jews would have been completely familiar with God's requirements from the OT Scriptures (cf. Prov. 5:15-20). Gentiles, too, in the first-century AD generally embraced conservative social behaviour in this respect.

Paul's first requirement for Titus' discernment is both biblical and practical. Even in today's society, where divorce and unfaithfulness are staggeringly common, there is still an undercurrent of disapproval for men

---

Unchristian behaviour caused huge (and unnecessary) rifts in the church in the United States during the twentieth century. *I strongly urge* those who might contemplate leaving their church to consider the words of Francis Schaeffer in *The Church Before the Watching World* in F. A. Schaeffer, *The Complete Works of Francis A. Schaeffer: A Christian Worldview.* second ed., 5 vols. (Wheaton, IL: Crossway, 1983), vol. 4, 151-63.

130 Doriani & Phillips, *2 Timothy and Titus*, 151, n. 3. Their commentary helpfully discusses the eligibility of single and divorced men for eldership, 151-53.

131 Yarbrough, *Letters to Timothy and Titus*, 480.

who leave their wives (and children) for another woman. Throughout Scripture it is God's intention that men should be faithful to one wife. This was reinforced by Jesus (Matt. 19:4-6). Even before Moses delivered the 'Ten Words' to Israel at Mount Sinai (Exodus 20), violation of this commandment brought dreadful consequences to offenders and others. One of the worst was Abraham's disobedience and lack of faith in his having sex with his wife's maid, Hagar, at his wife's suggestion (Gen. 16:1-3). The consequences of this sin are still felt today in the hostility between Arabs (Ishmael's descendants) and Jews (Isaac's descendants). King David's affair with Bathsheba caused the death of their child and a downward spiral in his kingship of Israel. The OT specifically endorses faithfulness in marriage through the emphasis in Proverbs 6:23-32.

Bray provides a detailed commentary on the issue of marriage concerning single and divorced men's eligibility for eldership. It probably wasn't much of an issue in Crete in the first century because of social disdain for divorce; however, Paul certainly does forbid polygamy. Most men in Cretan villages would have been married 'but it is hard to believe that a man would have been passed over for the eldership merely because he was single.'[132]

τέκνα ἔχων πιστά, μὴ ἐν κατηγορίᾳ ἀσωτίας ἢ ἀνυπότακτα. having believing children who are not open to the charge of being extravagant and disobedient.

This verse should not be interpreted as indicating the length of time that Christians had inhabited Crete, although we do know that Cretans were part of the large crowd that heard Peter preach at Pentecost (Acts 2:11). This would have been at least 30 years earlier than the date of this letter. But Guthrie notes that 'Bernard is nearer the truth

[132] G. L. Bray *The Pastoral Epistles*. ITC (London: T. & T. Clark, 2019), 478-79. See also Marshall with Towner, *The Pastoral Epistles*, 250-51; Mounce, *Pastoral Epistles*, 388.

when he understands the point to be that elders who have children are expected to have a Christian household.'[133] Bernard commented that the emphasis is on πιστά. It is not the fact that the ἐπίσκοπος has children that is important, but that if he has children, they should be professing Christians and of good behaviour. See 1 Tim. 3:4, 5 and the notes thereon.[134]

The mention of 'accusation' may suggest that these children would be adults,[135] although younger children would be expected to live in a household where godly discipline was enforced. These Christian children will display their faith by their works (Jas. 2:20). They will not be expected to be perfect, but they will refrain from being extravagant (ἀσωτία - *asōtia*).[136] The Greek word is associated with dissipation, the reckless spending of money (cf. 1 Pet. 4:4). The same behaviour (ἀσώτως) is represented in the story of the prodigal son (Luke 15:13; cf. Eph. 5:18; 1 Pet. 4:4). Neither should they be disobedient (ἀνυπότακτος - *anupotaktos*). The context probably refers to more than just disobedience to parents. This word connotes a sense of rebellion against society. See its use below in 1:10.

> Knight notes that the implication of ἔχων, 'having', children means that Paul is speaking 'only about children who are still rightfully under their father's authority in his home' (289). While this is a helpful insight as one seeks to apply the passage to the church, it is not dependent

---

[133] D Guthrie, *The Pastoral Epistles.* TNTC. Leicester: Inter-Varsity Press, 1957, 185.

[134] Bernard, *The Pastoral Epistles,* 157. It should be noted that Bernard was writing more than a century ago when social expectations of households were stricter than today. See also MacArthur, *1-2 Timothy and Titus,* 314; Yarbrough, *Letters to Timothy and Titus,* 481-83 for interpretations of children's expected behaviour.

[135] E F Scott, *The Pastoral Epistles.* MNTC (London: Hodder and Stoughton, 1936), 155. See Greenlee, *Titus and Philemon,* 27-8 for the variety of interpretations of these words.

[136] The NASB translation of 'wild' in 1:6 misses the underlying meaning of the word.

> on ἔχων as much as on the overall context that evaluates a man's ability to lead by looking at his management of his home. Yet the criterion is based not so much on the character of the children, regardless of where they live, as on a man's ability to manage his home, the results of which can be seen in his children wherever they live.[137]

Paul's requirements do not mean that elders must be married or have children. The apostle is making the point that, if elders are married, it must be to one wife. If they have young children, a Christian home with appropriate discipline is the type of environment that is required. If elders have adult children, their behaviour should be such as not to bring disrepute on their families. So it should be today.

1:7 in Detail

δεῖ γὰρ τὸν ἐπίσκοπον ἀνέγκλητον εἶναι ὡς θεοῦ οἰκονόμον
For it is necessary that the overseer must be blameless as a steward of God:

Paul's criteria for an elder find a parallel in his advice to Timothy (1 Tim. 3:1-10). He begins with those qualities an elder should not possess, followed by seven[138] positive personal qualifications.

The Greek words πρεσβυτέρος (*presbuteros*) in 1:5, 8 (also 1 Tim. 3:1) and ἐπίσκοπος (*episkopos*) in this verse have caused much unnecessary angst among Christians, ranging from theologians to laymen and everyone in between. The word *presbuteros* occurs seventy-two times in the NT, the majority being translated as 'elder'. It is derived from

[137] Mounce, *Pastoral Epistles*, 388. See also Bray, *The Pastoral Epistles*, 479, who suggests that Paul may have had in mind Eli and his two wicked sons, who brought downfall to the family (1 Samuel 2-4).

[138] The number seven reflects perfection in biblical literature. See its frequent use in Revelation.

πρεσβύτης (*presbutēs*), meaning 'an old man'. Although no men on Crete were 'old' in terms of faith in Christ, there is the implication that the future leaders of the Cretan churches would be older men, who presumably had more general wisdom and experience of life than young men.

The word *episkopos* only occurs five times in the NT. Its better meaning is 'overseer', a man having oversight of a congregation. Note that in v 7 Paul refers to '*an* overseer', clearly implying that these qualities are expected in all overseers. For the apostle to use both words as closely as he does in 1:5, 6, 7 we should conclude that these words are interchangeable in Paul's comments on those who will be appointed to church leadership. The later trend to call an overseer a 'bishop' (as opposed to 'elder') is inconsistent with the biblical text. Nevertheless, as early as the end of the first century AD, the term 'bishop' (in reference to one man as leader) was used by Ignatius of Antioch but the office is a human invention regardless of the piety and sincerity of those who originally used it. A useful summary of the relationship between 'overseers' and 'elders' at the time of this letter is provided by I. H. Marshall.[139]

For the purposes of understanding Paul's instructions in *Titus*, we should regard *presbuteros* and *episkopos* as synonymous. 'The similarity of the list to that in 1 Tim. 3:1-7, and the lack of any textual indication of change, suggests that Paul is discussing one office, not two, despite the shift from "elder" to "overseer."'[140] There is also a link between ἐπίσκοπος and οἰκονόμος (*oikonomos* – steward). The elder is to be one who takes care of things, as would a steward in a large estate (cf. Luke 12:42; Gal. 4:2). John MacArthur compares the role of elders (and pastors) to that of a shepherd, a lowly position in society then and

[139] See Marshall with Towner, *The Pastoral Epistles*, 170-81.

[140] Mounce, *Pastoral Epistles*, 385. See See Köstenberger, *Commentary on 1-2 Timothy and Titus*, 346. A lengthy examination of this issue (with whose conclusions I have some reservations) is provided in Bernard, *The Pastoral Epistles*, lvi-lxxv.

now.[141] Jesus used himself as an example of the Good Shepherd (cf. John 10:11-16; 21:15-17).

Once again, Paul lays stress on each leader being 'blameless'; 'a man of unimpeachable character' (NEB). 'He must be blameless in the matter of directing his own household (1:6) since his work will be to direct God's household.'[142] The need is reinforced by the special personal characteristics required of elders. Each is considered below.

The elder is a 'steward of *God*'. 'The commission of the ἐπίσκοπος is, in the end, from God and not from man; he is God's steward, the steward of His mysteries (1 Cor. 4:1) and of His manifold grace (1 Pet. 4:10), not, be it observed, the steward of the Christian community.

It is to God, not to man, that he is responsible for the due discharge of his office.'[143]

μὴ αὐθάδη,
not overbearing,

This is the person who seeks to dominate others, either by their power and/or authority or by the application of emotional pressure. The latter is perhaps more insidious because of its inconspicuous, crafty nature. The use of overt power or authority is easily recognised and can be combatted by an open challenge to its legitimacy. The word is derived from Greek meaning 'to please oneself'. 'Field notes that Aristotle (*Magn. Moral.* r. 28) counts **σεμνότης** as the mean between **αὐθάδεια** and **ἀρέσκεια, i.e. between arrogance on the one hand and over-complaisance** of manner on the other, an interesting observation.'[144] But subtle emotional manipulation is harder to

[141] See MacArthur, *1-2 Timothy and Titus*, 23-25.

[142] Greenlee, *Titus and Philemon*, 29.

[143] Bernard, *The Pastoral Epistles*, 158. See Fee *1 & 2 Timothy, Titus*, 173-74.

[144] Bernard, *The Pastoral Epistles*, 158 (original emphasis).

recognise and, therefore, expose. Another meaning of the word is 'self-opinionated'. In rejecting this personal characteristic Paul is again emphasising that elders must not undermine others by improper tactics or motives.

μὴ ὀργίλον,
not quick-tempered,

This is the only use of this word (ὀργίλος - *orgilos*) in the NT. However, LXX Proverbs 22:24-25 uses this word, cautioning that those who tolerate such a person only lay themselves open to 'learn his ways and find a snare for yourself' (cf. Prov. 29:8, 11, 22). A calm demeanour is a necessary qualification for an elder. John MacArthur notes that 'a qualified pastor must carefully guard against a spirit of hostility, resentment and anger. ... He can work with others in kindness, patience and gratitude.'[145] The bad example of King David's quick temper in 1 Samuel 25 demonstrates how potentially evil is this characteristic. He was saved from serious blood-guiltiness before God only because of the intervention of a wise woman.

μὴ πάροινον,
not given to drunkenness,

From the earliest records of human behaviour in the Bible (cf. Gen. 9:21) drunkenness has brought humans low. It was undoubtedly a social problem in the first century and remains a (probably worse) scourge today, compounded by the widespread use of drugs of addiction (both medically prescribed and illegally consumed). The modern social acceptance by many of the use of marihuana, heroin, cocaine, ice, etc. and excessive alcohol must be strenuously condemned by Christians. Paul's warning to the Ephesians (Eph. 5:18) cannot be emphasised too much in

---

[145] MacArthur, *1-2 Timothy and Titus*, 36.

the twenty-first century church, where liberal theology inevitably leads to liberal personal and social behaviour that does no credit to the gospel.

In this advice Paul is not forbidding the consumption of wine but drinking to the state where mental and/or physical impairment occurs. Elders must always be clear-headed and of sound judgment (cf. Prov. 31:4-5).

μὴ πλήκτην,
not violent,

This word refers primarily to physical altercations. Again, violence is continuously recorded as breaching God's will. Genesis 6:11 records that 'the earth was filled with violence'. So serious was this behaviour in God's eyes that he destroyed humanity (except for Noah and his family) with the flood. The unacceptability of violence by God (cf. Gen. 9:6) can never be tolerated by followers of the Prince of Peace (Is. 9:6; Acts 3:5), let alone leaders of his people. As well as physical fighting, much violence can be exercised by the tongue and, therefore, elders need to be restrained in their speech (cf. 2:8; Rom. 12:18).

μὴ αἰσχροκερδῆ,
not pursuing dishonest gain.

This disqualification for eldership should strike a resonant note in the western world. Time and again the media displays people who are pursuing dishonest gain, even in societies riven by poverty (cf. 1 Tim. 3:8; 1 Pet. 5:2). Its prevalence amongst the leaders of many 'mega-churches', especially in the United States, should be a cause of shame for the congregations that tolerate, let alone, participate in this grab for possessions.

Mounce is correct in his denunciation of this practice across all sectors of society. Paul basically condemns greed in general. See the use of κέρδος (*kerdos*) in 1:11.

> Barrett (129); followed by Fee (174) argues that this refers to making a profit from Christian service. But Paul has already established that Christian workers should make a living from their labours (1 Tim. 5:17-18), so Paul is referring to the desire to be rich beyond one's needs (cf. 1 Tim. 6:5-10, 17-19; Tit. 1:11).[146]

It is hardly surprising that Paul would adopt guidance from the Psalms and Wisdom literature (cf. Ps. 49:6; 62:10; Prov. 11:16; Eccles. 4:8) to emphasise the deceitfulness of greed.

1:8 in Detail

I urge readers to consult Yarbrough's commentary on this verse, where he explains clearly and at length the implications of Paul's requirements for those who might be contemplated for appointment as elders or pastors.[147] Paul moves from five vices to seven virtues.

ἀλλὰ φιλόξενον
Rather, he must be hospitable

Paul's emphatic use of ἀλλὰ (*alla* – rather [or '*but*']) turns his criteria from negative to positive. Elders must be hospitable. A practical NT example of its application is Gaius Titius Justus (Rom. 16:23), with whom Paul stayed in Corinth when writing his letter to the church in Rome. In the first century Christians travelling from place to place would have sometimes found it difficult to find accommodation that might be described as 'reputable'. How much more desirable would be the hospitality of fellow believers, if available. The following comment refers to Romans 16:23 but it is applicable to the situation that Titus would have found on Crete.

---

[146] Mounce, *Pastoral Epistles*, 390.
[147] Yarbrough, *Letters to Timothy and Titus*, 486-88.

> The term translated 'host' was used to refer both to a foreigner (e.g. Eph. 2:19) and to someone willing to extend hospitality to a foreigner. Plato, for example, could describe the custom by which a distinguished person might travel to another country, present himself to people of similar social standing there, and 'believing himself to be a proper guest [ξένος] for such a host [ξένῳ]' expect to receive a warm welcome (*Laws* 953d [G Bury, LCL]).
>
> Gaius was not merely a host to the foreigner Paul but to 'the whole church' (ὅλης τῆς ἐκκλησίας – *holēs tēs ekklēsias*). This phrase probably does not mean that Gaius accommodated in his supposedly large house an occasional plenary assembly of all the different, smaller house churches in Corinth. Since the term 'host' indicates that he was hospitable to foreigners, 'the whole church' had in mind the delegates from Macedonia, Asia, and Galatia who had assembled in Corinth to go with Paul and the collection to Jerusalem (cf. Acts 20:4). The term 'church' (ἐκκλησία), therefore, has the sense here of the worldwide fellowship of believers (cf. 1 Cor. 10:32; Gal. 1:13) rather than, as in Romans 16:1, 4, 5, and 16, the local 'assembly' of believers.[148]

This is an example of Christian hospitality. In a twenty-first century context, we know that hospitality takes many forms in many cultures. It's not difficult for any of us to extend hospitality to our friends and people we know and like. But what about strangers and people we don't like? That's a different issue! Throughout the Bible we see hospitality displayed in myriad situations. Abraham offered hospitality to three strangers who came to his tent (Gen. 18:1-8). It was Abigail's hospitality that prevented David from gross sin regarding her husband (1 Sam. 25:32-33).

[148] F. Thielman, *Romans*. ZECNT (Grand Rapids: Zondervan 2018), 743. For a contrary view, see J. D. G. Dunn, *Romans 9-16* (Dallas: Word Books, 1988), 910-11.

> Hospitality is not always as dramatic as meeting a policeman in your front door and accepting a visitor in the middle of the night. Sometimes it just making your home available for a Bible study, a church fellowship, or a party for your children and their friends. It can be having a quick cup of coffee with a coworker over a restaurant counter or serving an elegant dinner for dear friends. Whether in phone call, in a note, or during an impromptu conversation, hospitality can be as simple as a kind word or taking some time to really listen to another person. Whatever the means, the goal should be the same: to *encourage* others. …
>
> Hospitality is a ministry of encouragement. When we are willing to open our homes, our kitchens, our living rooms, and most of all our hearts to others, God can make exciting things happen.[149]

Jesus summarised this behaviour in Matthew 25:35-40.

φιλάγαθον
one who loves what is good

No doubt, Paul had in mind his advice in Philippians 4:8: 'Finally, brethren, whatever is true, whatever is honorable, whatever is right, whatever is pure, whatever is lovely, whatever is of good repute, if there is an excellence and if anything worthy of praise, dwell on these things.' This is the type of man who, in thought and action, is devoted to the well-being of others. The sense of what is 'good' ought to be applied in its widest possible context: personally, morally and regarding the world in general. Paul has more to say on this subject in 1:15.

σώφρονα
self-controlled

[149] Rachael Crabb with Raeann Hart, *The Personal Touch: Encouraging Others through Hospitality* (Colorado Springs, CO: NavPress, 1990), 17, 18.

This is the man who is disciplined to temperate behaviour, based on the exercise of sound judgment. A man who is clear-minded (sensible) (**σώφρονα** - *sōphrona*) thinks clearly, makes decisions with ease, and has a sense of mental sharpness. He has a clear understanding of his thoughts, emotions, and the present moment. Clarity helps people to define their goals, create a clear path to achieving them, and make effective decisions. Without clarity individuals may struggle with indecisiveness and a lack of direction and motivation (cf. Eccl. 7:9). 'Clarity of mind means clarity of passion, too; this is why a great and clear mind loves ardently and sees distinctly what it loves.'[150] See Bray's comments on *sōphrōn* in 2:2 below.[151] The opposite trait is ἀκρατής (*akratēs*), meaning 'a lack of self-control', as in 2 Timothy 3:3.

δίκαιον
upright

This characteristic is more than mere respectability. There is an implication in related Greek words that this elder would act justly. He is summarised in Psalm 24:3-4.

3 Who may ascend into the hill of the LORD? And who may stand in His holy place?
4 He who has clean hands and a pure heart,
Who has not lifted up his soul to falsehood
And has not sworn deceitfully.
NASB

This statement has been adopted in legal processes for centuries. In the law of equity (Australia, UK, USA and English law countries), it is a maxim that 'He who comes into equity must come with clean hands.' It is an equi-

150 Blaise Pascal.
151 See Marshall with Towner, *The Pastoral Epistles*, 182-93 for an examination of the σώφρων word-group and related concepts.

table defence for the defendant to argue that the plaintiff is not entitled to obtain an equitable remedy because the plaintiff is acting unethically or has acted in bad faith with respect to the subject of the complaint — that is, with 'unclean hands'. This is the sense of 'upright' in this word.

ὅσιον
holy

Although this Greek word is used eight times in the NT, with every occurrence in the NIV being translated 'holy', its context here means that the elder should be 'devout'. This, and the word above, compels the elder to live a fully Christian life in both the secular and religious aspects of his life.

> The word used here is not the one that typically describes sanctification, but the related word *hosion,* meaning 'a devout enthusiasm for piety and worship.' A qualified elder must love to worship in the congregation, as well as to honor God in family devotions. He must therefore also be 'disciplined,' especially when it comes to his personal practice of regular Bible reading, church attendance and prayer.[152]

ἐγκρατῆ
disciplined

The emphasis here, that an elder should be 'disciplined', not only applies to personal behaviour in his family or society. It is particularly relevant to his spiritual life personally and regarding the church that he helps to lead. 'It means to have strength to resist anything unjust or contrary to God's ordinances.'[153]

---

[152] Doriani & Phillips, *2 Timothy and Titus*, 155.
[153] Greenlee, *Titus and Philemon*, 32.

> 'Disciplined' in Paul's use here may serve to summarise the entire list of traits found in v 8: without the last one, the presence or absence of the previous five could quickly be rendered moot. It has been remarked that it takes twenty years to build a reputation, but only five minutes to destroy it.[154]

Only by regular knowledge of God's word and prayer will the elder be equipped to teach the gospel to others.

1:9 in Detail

ἀντεχόμενον τοῦ κατὰ τὴν διδαχὴν πιστοῦ λόγου,
He must hold firmly to the trustworthy message as it has been taught,

This instruction can be compared with Jude 3, where he writes about 'the faith once for all time entrusted to the saints.' The verb for 'hold firmly' (ἀντέχω - *antechō*) brings with it a sense of devotion to the truth (cf. Matt. 6:24; Luke 16:13 NIV) and a firm grasp of it (cf. Prov. 3:18). This gospel message is certain. Paul has preached this gospel through his entire ministry, having received it from God, 'who cannot lie' (1:2; cf. 1 Cor. 11:23). It is therefore completely trustworthy for everyone who hears it (see 3:8 for a repetition of πιστὸς λόγος (*pistos logos* - a trustworthy word). An elder must not depart from this truth and must instruct others regarding it. In 2:7 Paul describes the gospel as 'pure'. Zehr notes that 'to hold firmly to the trustworthy message as it has been taught' means 'understanding the whole Bible interpreted through God's fullness of revelation in Jesus Christ, as set forth by apostolic teaching.'[155]

---

[154] Yarbrough, *Letters to Timothy and Titus*, 488.
[155] P. M. Zehr, *1 & 2 Timothy, Titus*. Believers Church Bible Commentary (Scottdale, PA: Herald Press, 2010), 252.

ἵνα δυνατὸς ᾖ καὶ παρακαλεῖν ἐν τῇ διδασκαλίᾳ τῇ ὑγιαινούσῃ καὶ τοὺς ἀντιλέγοντας ἐλέγχειν.
so that he can encourage others by sound doctrine and refute those who oppose it.

The trustworthy message that Jesus came into the world to save sinners (1 Tim. 1:15) is how congregations can be encouraged and instructed by Titus' sound doctrine. However, Titus is to be aware that some will oppose or contradict (ἀντιλέγω – *antilegō*) his message. He is to refute (ἐλέγχω - e*legchō*) their claims. This word is also applied to slaves in 2:9. Calvin commented that 'A pastor needs two voices, one for gathering the sheep and the other for driving away wolves and thieves.' [156] It is a strong word for exposing and rebuking opponents. 'It means to show that they are wrong, to correct and reprove them, to convict them of their error, to enable them, if possible, to see their error and repent.'[157] Titus will have to use all his persuasive and ministerial skills (cf. 2 Corinthians 7-8) to encourage some (without losing their allegiance) while, at the same time, condemning false teaching.

Current Difficulties Within the Cretan Churches

1:10 *For there are many rebellious men, empty talkers and deceivers, especially those of the circumcision,*
1:11 *who must be silenced because they are upsetting whole families, teaching things they should not teach for the sake of sordid gain.*
1:12 *One of themselves, a prophet of their own, said, 'Cretans are always liars, evil beasts, lazy gluttons.'*

---

[156] J. Calvin, *The Second Epistle of Paul the Apostle to the Corinthians and the Epistles to Timothy, Titus and Philemon*. Trans. T. A. Smail. Eds. D. W. and T. F. Torrance (Grand Rapids: Eerdmans, 1964), 361.
[157] Greenlee, *Titus and Philemon*, 35.

1:13 *This testimony is true. For this reason reprove them severely so that they may be sound in the faith,*

1:14 *not paying attention to Jewish myths and commandments of men who turn away from the truth.*

1:15 *To the pure, all things are pure; but to those who are defiled and unbelieving, nothing is pure, but both their mind and their conscience are defiled.*

1:16 *They profess to know God, but by their deeds they deny Him, being detestable and disobedient and worthless for any good deed.*
NASB

Paul never equivocates in his condemnation of those who oppose the gospel. In vv 10-16 he describes clearly those with whom Titus will have to deal. This reflects his writing in 1 Timothy 3:1-7 on gospel opponents. There is criticism of some Cretans, whose teaching and behaviour are contrary to gospel imperatives.

> In a sense the substance of the whole epistle turns on this section [1:10-16]. It goes far toward explaining just why Paul is writing. We have already seen that a major aim is to support Titus in his mission of completing unfinished business in the Cretan churches and appointing elders (1:5). To that end Paul has given a concise but rich description of desirable qualities in pastoral candidates (1:6-9). He will subsequently set forth desirable qualities among various groups in the congregations (2:1-10) and explain why Titus' outreach to various groups holds such urgency and promise (2:11-15). Finally, he will give general directives for all believers (3:1-3), a rationale for their actions (3:4-8), and final warnings regarding controversies in the churches (3:9-11).[158]

[158] Yarbrough, *Letters to Timothy and Titus*, 490.

1:10 in Detail

εἰσὶν γὰρ πολλοὶ [καὶ] ἀνυπότακτοι, ματαιολόγοι καὶ φρεναπάται,
For there are many rebellious people, full of meaningless talk and deception,

Paul's expectations in vv 5-9 of the personal qualities of the future Cretan elders are both appropriate from a Christian perspective yet ambitious from a worldly perspective. The practical difficulties are faced in vv 10-16. It needs to be remembered that the following descriptions are not of Cretans generally (although that may sometimes be the case in practice) but of some in the then-existing Cretan churches from whom elders would need to be selected.

By commencing with γὰρ (*gar* — for), Paul gives the reasons for his insistence on the selection of men with unblemished character. The reason is, disturbingly, that there are *many* (πολλοὶ - *polloi*) rebellious (ἀνυπότακτοι-*anupotaktoi*) people. This word is already used in 1:6 to denounce such behaviour amongst the children of potential elders. Rebels want to overturn authority. Numbers are unknown but it seems clear that there were more than one or two prominent troublemakers. It only takes ten or so people in different congregations to stir up strife amongst many more. This rebelliousness is repeated by Paul in 1 Timothy 1:9 where he states that 'the law is made not for the righteous but lawbreakers and rebels.'

> Yet, the thrust of the word is hardly obscure — the people it describes are out of line, in Paul's view, with norms they should respect — and in any case Paul gives further qualification. He spotlights first what they do, and next who they are.[159]

---

[159] Yarbrough, *Letters to Timothy and Titus*, 492. See Doriani & Phillips, *2 Timothy and Titus*, 146, 162-63.

The rebellion espoused by these troublers is 'full of meaningless talk and deception'. Using contemporary language, Zerwick and Grosvenor translate ματαιολόγοι (*mataiologoi*) as 'windbags', those who speak nonsense (cf. 1 Tim. 1:6). It is a NT *hapax*. Others fall into the category of φρεναπάται (*phrenapatai*), 'self-deceivers' (cf. Gal. 6:3), those who are fooling themselves. Nevertheless, if there are people in churches speaking nonsense or deluded thoughts, some will take notice and error will spread.

The spread of liberal theology through much of the Church in the western world is a cancer that is destroying the body of Christ. We need courageous men to declare the gospel of Jesus Christ openly and, at the same time, expose and rebut false teaching ('meaningless talk and deception') and unchristian behaviour that is becoming so prevalent and fashionable, be it from the pulpit, congregation or theological colleges. This why elders, now and then, must be self-controlled, upright, devout and disciplined (1:8).

> Clearly for Paul appointing qualified leaders was at the top of his priority list when it came to church planting. In this regard Paul led by example, mentoring numerous men in what has come to be known as the 'Pauline circle.' Jesus, too, devoted most of his time on earth to leadership training and development (the Twelve). Today we neglect giving proper attention to leadership issues in the church at our peril and the church's detriment. Not only will the church, God's household, not be properly led and managed, but it will also be rendered vulnerable to the influence of false teaching, worldliness, and a variety of countervailing cultural and social trends.[160]

μάλιστα οἱ ἐκ τῆς περιτομῆς,
especially those of the circumcision group.

[160] MacArthur, *1-2 Timothy and Titus*, 316.

By using μάλιστα (*malista* – 'especially'), Paul wants Titus to concentrate on one particular group of troublemakers. Here, the majority of the offenders are named: οἱ ἐκ τῆς περιτομῆς (*hoi ek tēs peritomēs*): those from the 'circumcision group', the Jews (from within the church). Weiland examines this phrase and notes that 'In the same expression in Gal. 2.12 Dunn discerns "an identity determined by or focused on the act and fact of circumcision—hence the metonymy 'the circumcision', not 'the circumcised', indicating a specific faction within Judaism"'.[161] We recall that Christianity was not unknown to Crete before Paul and Titus undertook their first missionary journey on the island. Acts 2:11 records that some Cretans heard Peter's first sermon at Pentecost in Jerusalem. Undoubtedly, they were Jews attending the Feast of the Passover and it is reasonable to assume that some were converted to this 'new way' and took the gospel of Jesus home with them. So we can assume that a fragmentary version of the gospel had circulated in Crete for approximately 30 years before Paul wrote to Titus. We do not know the extent (if any) of subsequent teaching about Jesus and the gospel of grace. The strong reference to 'the circumcision group' (some Jews) may reflect a Jewishness that would not accept Jesus as the Christ.[162] No doubt, the missionary journey of Paul and Titus could have fanned the flames of faith in those early believers as well as converting some Cretans. However, by the time of this letter, Paul discerned that Cretan Jews were one of the main obstacles to the progress of the gospel in the churches. We do not know the numbers of Jews and Gentiles in the Cretan churches. However, Fee claims

161 Weiland, 'Roman Crete', 352. See J. D. G. Dunn, 'Echoes of Intra-Jewish Polemic in Paul's Letter to the Galatians', *JBL* 112:3 (1993): 459-77, 461.

162 Mounce, *Pastoral Epistles*, 383.

that historical evidence points to 'a large number of Jews on Crete.'[163]

It is quite possible that, during Paul's evangelistic visit, many of these Jews had either misunderstood Paul's gospel of justification by faith in Jesus without the need for compliance with the Mosaic Law or that they simply ignored it and carried on with ancient Jewish religious practices. As Paul knew from his critical encounter with Peter in Antioch (cf. Gal. 2:11-14), it was intolerable for Christian Jews to continue with adherence to the Law when Christ's death and resurrection had abolished that need (cf. Romans 4). This 'meaningless talk and deception' had to be addressed in the strongest possible way.

1:11 in Detail

οὓς δεῖ ἐπιστομίζειν, οἵτινες ὅλους οἴκους ἀνατρέπουσιν διδάσκοντες ἃ μὴ δεῖ αἰσχροῦ κέρδους χάριν.
They must be silenced, because they are disrupting whole households by teaching things they ought not to teach – and that for the sake of dishonest gain.

Paul is emphatic. 'They must be silenced!' This is no longer a private matter. They must be publicly refuted and probably be subject to discipline by the church.[164] Two reasons are given. First, they are causing severe disturbances to 'whole households'. The verb used by Paul for this disruption (ἀνατρέπω - *anatrepō*) is the same used in John 2:15 when Jesus overturned the tables of the money changers. 'The literal meaning of this verb is "overturn," but it is used here figuratively in the sense of upsetting or ruining someone's beliefs or opinions. See 2 Tim. 2:18.'[165] Serious conflict is arising. The Greek text suggests that

[163] Fee, *1 & 2 Timothy, Titus*, 183. See Yarbrough, *Letters to Timothy and Titus*, 493.
[164] Doriani & Phillips, *2 Timothy and Titus*, 165.
[165] Perkins, *The Pastoral Letters*, 253.

the false teaching and the disruption of households is contemporaneous.

> The 'upset' in mind is almost certainly the defection of entire families to the false teachers, or the destruction of the faith once professed by members of a household by the false teaching such as 2 Tim. 2:18 and 1 Tim. 1:20 envisage. Alternatively, since it was typical for the church to meet in houses, it is possible that the reference is to the capitulation of whole house churches.[166]

Secondly, and even worse, is that these Jews are receiving dishonest gain (αἰσχρός κέρδος – *aischros kerdos*) for their warped teaching (cf. 1:7). These 'teachers' are not interested in the truth of the gospel or the wellbeing of their hearers: they are just doing this for money. The greed of Cretans for money was well known throughout the ancient world. Polybius commented that, 'So much in fact do sordid love of gain and lust for wealth prevail among them, that the Cretans are the only people in the world in whose eyes no gain is disgraceful.'[167]

1:12 in Detail

εἶπέν τις ἐξ αὐτῶν, ἴδιος αὐτῶν προφήτης, κρῆτες ἀεὶ ψεῦσται, κακὰ θηρία, γαστέρες ἀργαί.
One of Crete's own prophets has said it: 'Cretans are always liars, evil brutes, lazy gluttons.'

Now comes a severe condemnation of Cretan society as a whole using an ancient stereotype. The saying is claimed to go back to a Cretan poet (some of whom were regarded

---

[166] Marshall with Towner, *The Pastoral Epistles*, 197. See Fee *1 & 2 Timothy, Titus*, 178: 'In some cases **whole households** are being overturned by the false teachers, rather than, as some have suggested, some families being upset by the defection of one or two within them.' (original emphasis)

[167] Polybius, *Histories (6.46.3)*, Loeb Classical Library.

as 'prophets' in Greco-Roman culture) named Epimenides around 500 BC.[168] This condemnation related to the fact that Cretans claimed that the Greek god Zeus was buried in Crete; whereas, in Greek mythology, he was very much alive! 'So notorious were the Cretans that the Greek language developed a verb, *kretzio,* based on their name to signify lying and cheating.'[169] Köstenberger does not take Paul's comment lightly and the strength of his comments regarding *both* Jews and Cretans may well speak to the moral degeneration of our current western society where such traits seem to be coming all too common.

> [t]he Jew and the Cretan had something in common. The employment of trickery or deception for selfish advantage characterised both (cf. John 1:47 with Tit. 1:12). An honest Jew or an honest Cretan seems to have been an exception. And certainly the combination *Cretan-Jew* was not a happy one.
>
> The expression 'evil brutes' describes the savage and cruel character of the Cretans of the days of Epimenedes and of the days of Paul and Titus. They would push everyone out of the way in order to gain an advantage for themselves.
>
> The Cretans, then, are *untruthful, selfish* and *pleasure-loving*. Now some writers consider the action of Paul in quoting this devastating verdict with respect to the character of the Cretans as singularly untactful, a 'smear' upon the good name of an entire population. However, the character of the Cretans displayed itself so clearly that confirmation of the severe judgment comes from every direction and is not limited to a single century. The reader should see this for himself. In addition to the noun 'Cretism' = *lie,* and to the verb 'to Cretise' = *to deceive, to tell lies.*[170]

---

168 See MacArthur, *1-2 Timothy and Titus,* 319, n. 81 for a lengthy discussion on the background to this saying. See also Mounce, *Pastoral Epistles,* 397-99.

169 Doriani & Phillips, *2 Timothy and Titus,* 164.

170 Köstenberger, *Commentary on 1-2 Timothy and Titus,* 352-53.

Köstenberger lists historical quotes from ancient historians from 200 BC to AD 100. No wonder that Paul writes that this condemnation is true. While it would be true that Paul was not condemning every Cretan, let alone all Cretan Christians, he is simply informing Titus of the social environment in which he lives and, accordingly, must act with wisdom and discretion. Although Crete was famous for not possessing any wild animals,[171] it certainly had wild people, who were undisciplined, liars and criminals.

1:13 in Detail

ἡ μαρτυρία αὕτη ἐστὶν ἀληθής. δι᾽ ἣν αἰτίαν ἔλεγχε αὐτοὺς ἀποτόμως, ἵνα ὑγιαίνωσιν ἐν τῇ πίστει,
This saying is true. Therefore rebuke them sharply, so that they will be sound in the faith

Paul's confirmation of the general validity of this societal condemnation reflects his awareness of the Cretan people, not only from his short missionary journey there but also his broad life experience during his ministry in Greece. '[e]very minister of the gospel must of necessity be cognizant with the character of his people, however distasteful the facts may be.'[172] Having already instructed Titus to 'silence them', he continues his opposition by insisting: ἔλεγχε ἀποτόμως (*elenche apotomōs*) 'reprimand them sharply' (cf. 2 Cor. 13:10). ἀποτόμως is derived from the verb τέμνω (temnō – to cut), indicating that Titus' criticism would be severe. This is the only occasion in the letter where Paul instructs Titus personally to rebuke the false teachers. ἐλέγχω (*elenchō*) is a strong verb for finding fault (cf. Jude 15; Rev. 3:19). But there is a reason for this. Such discipline emphasises what truth comprises, appro-

171 Quinn, *The Letter to Titus*, 108.
172 Guthrie, *The Pastoral Epistles*, 188.

priately corrects overt misbehaviour and is a warning to all the congregations to maintain soundness of doctrine and practise. They are currently not 'sound in the faith' but, hopefully, this sharp rebuke will get them into line. However, there are specific faults that Paul emphasises, especially concerning many of the Jews in the congregations. Titus' criticism of the false teachers may also have the spillover effect that the believing Christians are also put on notice about what is right and wrong doctrinally.

Yarbrough makes the interesting point: '"They" could possibly refer, not to the troublemakers, but to those in the church they threaten to subvert. Then Paul's command would be especially for the sake of those who stand in the way of the harm the troublemakers can inflict.'[173]

1:14 in Detail

μὴ προσέχοντες ἰουδαϊκοῖς μύθοις καὶ ἐντολαῖς ἀνθρώπων ἀποστρεφομένων τὴν ἀλήθειαν.
and will pay no attention to Jewish myths or to the merely human commands of those who reject the truth.

προσέχοντες (*prosechontes*) is the present active participle of ρροσέχω (*prosechō*), meaning 'to pay attention to'. μὴ (*mē*) negates the verb. The use of the present tense means that there are people who habitually turn away from the truth. Quinn describes these 'myths' (cf. 2 Tim. 4:4).

> Myths were not just stories, or just stories about what had never really occurred; they were stories in which … their authors foisted their own immoral conduct on the gods or … enticed their hearers into evil acts on divine precedents.'[174]

[173] Yarbrough, *Letters to Timothy and Titus*, 497.
[174] Quinn, *The Letter to Titus*, 110-12.

Paul's directive 'means primarily that they should stop paying attention to these false teachings if they are listening to them, and also that they should not pay attention to them if they have not already done so.'[175] Nor should believers pay any attention to the 'merely human commands' that probably concern food, marriage, and Jewish rites and customs because they are inconsistent Christian teaching (cf. 1 Tim. 1:4; Col. 2:20-23 discusses 'the commandments and teachings of men'). These people reject the truth.

> It is the 'fightings about the law' that are pronounced in the Epistle to Titus to be 'unprofitable and vain' (Tit. 3:9). Thus, whatever the growth of the heresy may have been like, it had its roots in Judaism. We are not, of course, to confuse these apostles of novelty with the Judaising opponents whom St Paul had to face in earlier years. There is nothing here of any insistence upon circumcision, or upon the perpetual obligations of the Mosaic law. That is now a thing of the past within the Christian Society. Christianity had won for itself a position independent of Judaism, though no doubt its independence would only be fully appreciated by its own adherents. To the eye of a stranger Christianity was still a Jewish sect. But it was not so counted by Christians themselves. Jewish thought would necessarily influence men brought up in the atmosphere of the synagogue and the temple, but the influence would hardly be consciously felt. And we find that the opposition which Timothy and Titus were to offer to the novel doctrines that were gaining popularity, was suggested not because the doctrines were Jewish, but because they were fabulous and unedifying.[176]

The Cretans must not pay attention to merely human commands *of those who reject* (ἀποστρέφω – *apostrephō*) *the truth* (my emphasis) (cf. Col. 2:21-22). This word is used

[175] Greenlee, *Titus and Philemon*, 42.

[176] Bernard, *The Pastoral Epistles*, xlviii.

nine times in the NT and on each occasion it refers to 'turning back' to former ways (cf. Matt. 5:42; Heb. 12:25). Godly commands should be obeyed. It is important to distinguish between the two groups mentioned by Yarbrough above in his comment on 'they' in this verse. Paul is drawing a clear distinction between *divine* authority (the gospel) and *human* 'commands'. There is no place whatsoever for human ideas or commands (let alone requirements) to contradict or supersede the authority of Scripture. Jesus had warned about this: 'You neglect the commandment of God, in order to maintain the tradition of men' (Mark 7:8 NEB).

1:15 in Detail

πάντα καθαρὰ τοῖς καθαροῖς· τοῖς δὲ μεμιαμμένοις καὶ ἀπίστοις οὐδὲν καθαρόν, ἀλλὰ μεμίανται αὐτῶν καὶ ὁ νοῦς καὶ ἡ συνείδησις.
To the pure, all things are pure, but to those who are corrupted and do not believe, nothing is pure. In fact, both their minds and consciences are corrupted.

This is a restatement of Jesus' teaching in Mark 7:15 that 'there is nothing outside the man which can defile him if it goes into him; but the things which proceed out of the man are what defile the man' (cf. Rom. 14:20). *Spiritual* pollution comes from within a person, not without. Rituals and contact with 'impure' things do not make a person 'impure'. The word 'pure' (καθαρός – *katharos*) 'has two meanings: it has a ritual or ceremonial meaning when referring to all things, and a moral meaning when referring to people.'[177]

> The fact that Paul has been thinking of the opponents' ascetic teachings now comes to the forefront. To under-

[177] Greenlee, *Titus and Philemon*, 43.

stand v 15 one must see that Paul is using καθαρός 'clean,' in two different ways, referring to both ritual and moral purity. Here he says that 'all things are [ritually] clean to the [morally] clean.' The first 'clean' (καθαρὰ) must refer to ritual purity since not all things are morally pure. The second 'clean' (καθαρο ῖς) must refer to moral purity because ritual purity is inconsequential (Mark 7:7). This was the experience of Peter in Acts 10:15, 34-35 (cf. 15:9). Paul's Jewish Christian opponents would have been teaching that a morally pure person is still made unclean by eating unclean foods or by touching any defiled thing (cf. Hag. 2:10-14; Philo *Spec. Leg.* 3.208-9). This topic has already been discussed in 1 Timothy 4:1-5 where Paul asserts that all things are clean because God created them good, and the same topic is raised here for Titus' sake.[178]

'The real seat of purity is the *conscience* and if defilement has entered there, *mind* and action are alike affected.'[179]

1:16 in Detail

θεὸν ὁμολογοῦσιν εἰδέναι, τοῖς δὲ ἔργοις ἀρνοῦνται, βδελυκτοὶ ὄντες καὶ ἀπειθεῖς καὶ πρὸς πᾶν ἔργον ἀγαθὸν ἀδόκιμοι.

They claim to know God, but by their actions they deny him. They are detestable, disobedient and unfit for doing anything good.

Titus 1:16 is the hinge verse of the entire epistle. The opponents claimed to know God, but their godless lives showed that they did not, and as a result they were not living out their salvation as God intended, pursuing good works. The essence of the Cretan theology was that they thought belief and practice could be separated, and Paul spends

[178] Mounce, *Pastoral Epistles*, 400.

[179] Guthrie, *The Pastoral Epistles*, 190 (original emphasis). See Marshall with Towner, *The Pastoral Epistles*, 207-11.

> most of the rest of the letter arguing that God's salvific work and the believer's life of obedience must go hand in hand. Of course, this zeal for good works commended by Paul cannot earn salvation, but it is the necessary corollary to God's salvation and is in line with his original intent. [180]

They *claim* (ὁμολογέω – *homologeō*) to know God. This verb is 'a technical term for confessing Christ'[181] and is generally used in the NT to make a confession of faith or belief (cf. Luke 12:8; Rom. 10:9) but here Paul is exposing these Judaisers as being liars in their words, which are confirmed by their actions. Their behaviour exposed the lack of sincerity in what they claimed to believe, as was the case in *Jude*.

Strong words follow, as in Galatians 5:12, reflecting the intensity of Paul's feeling towards those who reject or attempt to pervert the gospel. These men are 'detestable'[182] (βδελυκτός – *bdeluktos*), a NT *hapax*. It is a word frequently used in the LXX 'to describe that which is detestable to God, especially idolatry.'[183] They are 'intractable'[184] (ἀπειθής – *apeithēs*), (the worst type of people in a prison) and have failed the test (ἀδόκιμος – *adokimos*) (cf. 2 Cor. 13:5); i.e. they are below standard and unfit for anything good in the Christian community.

This complete condemnation of the Judaisers (and anyone else who disputes Paul's teachings) informs Titus of the strength and error of his opponents' arguments and their tenacity to maintain their position. Titus will need courage and wisdom to combat these opponents.

---

180 Mounce, *Pastoral Epistles*, 395.

181 Mounce, *Pastoral Epistles*, 402.

182 Zerwick and Grosvenor, *Analysis of the Greek New Testament*, vol. 2, 648 translate this as 'abominable'.

183 Mounce, *Pastoral Epistles*, 403.

184 Zerwick and Grosvenor, *Analysis of the Greek New Testament*, vol. 2, 648.

CHAPTER 2

Teaching and Behaviour for Various Groups

2:1 *But as for you, speak the things which are fitting for sound doctrine.*
2:2 *Older men are to be temperate, dignified, sensible, sound in faith, in love, in perseverance.*
2:3 *Older women likewise are to be reverent in their behaviour, not malicious gossips nor enslaved to much wine, teaching what is good,*
2:4 *so that they may encourage the young women to love their husbands, to love their children,*
2:5 *to be sensible, pure, workers at home, kind, being subject to their own husbands, so that the word of God will not be dishonored.*
2:6 *Likewise urge the young men to be sensible;*
NASB

Thus the concern throughout the passage is on observable behaviour, obviously in contrast to that of the 'opponents' described in 1:10-16, who are finally judged as unqualified for any good work. The language used is quite general and very much that which was current in pagan philosophical and religious circles, here adapted to Christian life. One gets the feeling, therefore, that the passage does not so much address *ad hoc* problems in Crete as it does in a more general way call for good works and a lifestyle on the part of Christians that will make the teaching about God our Saviour attractive (v 10).[185]

Christians of both sexes and all ages are urged to consider their conduct before the watching world, as well as towards one another.[186]

2:1 in Detail

σὺ δὲ λάλει ἃ πρέπει τῇ ὑγιαινούσῃ διδασκαλίᾳ.
But as for you, speak the things which are fitting for sound doctrine.

A strong reaction in the opposite direction comes from Paul to Titus. Notwithstanding the opponents whom he would encounter, Paul now addresses Titus personally: '**But as for you**' (σὺ δὲ - *su de*). He similarly addresses Timothy in 1 Timothy 6:11; 2 Timothy 2:1; 3:14; 4:5, 15. In 1:5 Paul tells Titus why he left him in Crete and what he needed to do. This chapter is a continuation of those tasks. Part of Titus' responsibility is speaking (including teaching) — a completely contrary position to the false teaching that proliferates. Paul discusses key issues for various groups within the churches. 'In requiring each of the groups to observe a high standard of conduct, he is concerned as much for the good reputation of the church as for the furtherance of the gospel in an environment of doubtful morality.'[187] All of them are to be based on 'sound doctrine' (ὑγιαινούσῃ διδασκαλίᾳ - *hugiainousē didaskalia*), which are the same words relevant to the instruction required of elders. Note the linguistic link between two Greek words for 'sound'

[185] Fee *1 & 2 Timothy, Titus*, 184.
[186] See Fee *1 & 2 Timothy, Titus*, 185.
[187] Kelly, *A Commentary on the Pastoral Epistles*, 239.

and 'holy'. It is used again in the following verse. Clearly, the appointing of elders was a priority if sound doctrine was to be disseminated more widely.

In this letter Paul does not use the Greek words for 'teach' and 'preach'. Rather, he refers to what Titus should 'say' or 'speak', as in this verse. Much of Titus' speech would be directed to imparting sound doctrine and behavioural imperatives; therefore, it would mainly be in the form of teaching. We do not need to have specific words to know that Titus' main task with the new elders and their congregations would be teaching. However, 'Paul's concern is not limited to what Titus "teaches" or preaches in the formal sense but extends to *the fullest expression of who he is as a verbal and interactive man of faith and ecclesiastical leader* .'[188] (cf. Matt. 12:34).

2:2 in Detail

πρεσβύτας νηφαλίους εἶναι, σεμνούς, σώφρονας, ὑγιαίνοντας τῇ πίστει, τῇ ἀγάπῃ, τῇ ὑπομονῇ.
Older men are to be worthy of respect, temperate, self-controlled, sound in faith, in love, in perseverance.

Paul is not relying on Cretan customs or culture when he sets forth the following behavioural characteristics for Cretan Christians. He is following his own earlier apostolic instructions to churches in Greece and Asia, based on accepted OT Scriptures and Jesus' sayings. This is supposed to be distinctly Christian behaviour. If it happens to coincide with some current Cretan social practices, well and good, but the requirements of the gospel must come first.[189]

---

[188] Yarbrough, *Letters to Timothy and Titus*, 507-08, 510 (my emphasis). See also Mounce, *Pastoral Epistles*, 408.

[189] See Yarbrough, *Letters to Timothy and Titus*, 508.

In this verse πρεσβύτης (*presbutēs*) refers, not to elders but to ***older men***, although this word does provide clues about those more likely to be appointed elders: mature men with characters like those described in 1:6-9. It is a rare NT word, used only by Paul of himself (Phlm. 9) and by Luke of Zechariah, the father of John the Baptist (Luke 1:8). This group should be addressed first because, in most cultures of the time, older men were the leaders of their communities and accorded appropriate respect (νηφαλίος - *nēphalios*). These were probably men older than fifty years of age.[190] Paul goes further by requiring them to be 'worthy of respect' (σεμνός - *semnos*); i.e. dignified and self-controlled (σώφρων - *sōphrōn*). This also applies to women (cf. 1 Tim. 3:8, 11). The need for all men (especially older ones) to be 'sensible' (see 1:8 for the same word used for 'clear-minded') is obvious; see 2:6 below.

Gerald Bray has helpful comments about these three qualities.

> The first of these qualities sets the tone for the other two, which have to be understood in relation to it. As is generally the case in Greek, the full meaning of the adjectives is almost impossible to convey in a single word. This means that although the translations describe some aspects of what Paul meant, they do not capture the whole meaning. A ***nēphalios*** was a man who exercised sound judgment based on a dispassionate consideration of the facts and circumstances. He was not the kind of person who would be swept away by his own passions or inclined to show favouritism for unworthy motives. A ***semnos*** was someone whose conduct matched his profession of faith. This was a man who did what was expected of him, who played his part in a way that earned general respect and who did not behave in ways that were inconsistent with his standing in the community.
>
> Finally, an old man had to be ***sōphrōn***. This impossible-to-translate word was an essential virtue in ancient

[190] Quinn, *The Letter to Titus*, 129.

> Greece and one of the main goals of all education. It certainly involved 'self-control,' which is how it is often translated, but it was more than that. A *sōphrōn* was someone who was wise in a practical way and balanced in his behaviour. He maintained his cool in the most trying of circumstances, was slow to react and eschewed judgments based on emotion rather than on reason. He was not deceived by appearances or swayed by personal preferences that might cloud his decisions and make him appear erratic or biased in the eyes of others.[191]

Three further requirements are stated for older Christian men: to be sound in faith, love (cf. 1 Tim. 1:5; 6:11) and perseverance (cf. 1 Tim. 6:11). On ὑγιαίνοντας (*hugiainontas*), Perkins comments: 'This participle here and in Titus 1:13 qualifies believers. This usage implies a contrast with old men who confess to be Christian but are not sound in faith, love, and endurance.'[192] These are foundational Christian virtues, without which the elders will find it difficult to maintain sound doctrine and behaviour. Additionally, all older men should strive for this sort of character.

These comments are particularly relevant to the twenty-first century church and should part of the assessment of men called to be elders today.

> All the above-mentioned traits are marks of spiritual and personal maturity that should characterize an older person in the faith. Blessed is the church that has among its members such older men who can serve as models of dignity, respectability and wisdom.[193]

---

[191] Bray, *The Pastoral Epistles*, 503. See Bernard, *The Pastoral Epistles*, 45, 53.

[192] Perkins, *The Pastoral Letters*, 259.

[193] Köstenberger, *1–2 Timothy & Titus*, 330.

2:3 in Detail

πρεσβύτιδας ὡσαύτως ἐν καταστήματι ἱεροπρεπεῖς, μὴ διαβόλους μὴ οἴνῳ πολλῷ δεδουλωμένας, καλοδιδασκάλους, Older women likewise are to be reverent in their behaviour, not malicious gossips nor enslaved to much wine, teaching what is good,

As with the older men, older women are 'likewise' (ὡσαύτως - *hōsautōs*) to be encouraged to adopt positive behaviour and act as role models to younger women. The older women were to be treated as seriously as the older men. Older Christians have a responsibility to younger Christians. Commenting on their behaviour, Köstenberger notes that 'it's unusual that the role of the older women is cast in almost priestly terms (ἱεροπρεπεῖς, v 3).'[194] Quinn comments that Titus 2:3-4a has 'terminology practically unexampled in this correspondence or in biblical Greek.'[195] It is clear from this adjective that Titus must exhort the older women to attain for high standards in their ministry to younger women.

It is well known that most women in the first century AD spent most of their time and activities around their homes. From a practical perspective, their behaviour mattered because it would be observed by all: neighbours and family. Gossiping (διαβόλος - *diabolos*) has always been condemned in Scripture (cf. Prov. 20:19), and Paul will not tolerate it. Relevantly, he uses the same word against this practice to Timothy (cf. 1 Tim. 3:11; 2 Tim. 3:3). From this Greek word we derive 'diabolical' in English and 'devil' in Spanish. It is a particularly female attribute, which could cause huge dissension in small groups like the Cretan churches. Even today, all readers will be familiar with the disastrous effects of gossiping and there is the

---

194 Köstenberger, *1–2 Timothy & Titus*, 331.
195 Quinn, *Titus*, 134.

need for godly older women to refrain from it and to teach younger women of its insidious worming into otherwise united groups.

There is a warning for older women, which must have occurred to Paul from his actual experience of seeing society while travelling in Crete. The most common word in the NT for 'wine' is οἶνος (*oinos*) but Paul includes it in a phrase μὴ οἴνῳ πολλῷ δεδουλωμένας (*mē oinō pollō dedoulōmenas*). The last Greek word is less common in the NT and derives from δοῦλος (*doulos*), meaning 'a slave'. It is apparent that Paul saw many older women (probably in Cretan society in general) who were enslaved (addicted) to wine, apparently a problem in both Hellenistic and Jewish societies.[196]

Quite contrary to this sordid impression, the older women should resort to teaching what is good (καλοδιδασκάλος - *kalodidaskalos*). Although a NT *hapax*, Köstenberger regards it as 'apparently a Pauline coinage'.[197] This teaching would not occur in public assemblies, but in private as per Lois and Eunice (2 Tim 3:15).[198]

> NIV translates '*but* to teach what is good.' The italicized word, absent in Greek, is a reasonable inference, given the flow of the discourse: the women should not be slanderers or drunks *but* teachers of the good. Few if any other translations (but see NLT) interpolate the adversative conjunction, the effect of which may be to place additional emphasis on the wine and speech problems and give the discourse a slightly moralistic tone — as if not slandering others or sousing oneself is tantamount to teaching what is good. Too much should not be made of the presence or absence of an adversative. But without 'but' it may be clearer that Paul values the actual teaching role (not just the absence of gossip and drunkenness) in women

---

196 See P. M. Zehr, *1 & 2 Timothy, Titus,* Believers Church Bible Commentary (Scottdale, PA: Herald Press, 2010), 265.

197 Köstenberger, *1–2 Timothy & Titus*, 330.

198 Bernard, *The Pastoral Epistles*, 166.

> who have reached the level of maturity assumed here. Translations taking this tack often begin a new sentence that underscores this emphasis: 'They are to teach what is good' (ESV, RSV, NRSV, CSB); 'They must teach what is proper' (CEV; cf. JB, NEB).[199]

2:4 in Detail

ἵνα σωφρονίζωσιν τὰς νέας φιλάνδρους εἶναι, φιλοτέκνους, so that they may urge the young women to love their husbands, to love their children,

Again, we see the appearance of *sōphrōn* in σωφρονίζωσιν (*sōphrōnizōsin*). It is a Greek value to which everyone (especially older people) should aspire. There is always a practical point in Paul's advice. This time it is the reason for reverential behaviour by the older women.

> The entire word group of which the verb 'urge' is part is redolent of qualities like prudence, moderation, good judgment, reasonableness, rationality, and self-control. With the verb in v 4 Paul urges Titus to steer older women toward inculcating certain admirable and beneficial qualities in younger women, not to 'train' them in rote formalities, mere external actions, or (as the household code theory has it) cultural accommodation.[200]

The outcome is encouragement for the younger women to love their husbands (φιλάνδρος - *philandros*) and children (φιλοτέκνος - *philoteknos*) (cf. 1:11). Both words are NT *hapaxes*. Paul does not use the normal Christian word for love, ἀπάπη (*agapē*) but φιλος (*philos*), a word relevant to affection between family, friends and society. Paul appears not to be concerned with romantic love but a deep care and concern for one's immedi-

[199] Yarbrough, *Letters to Timothy and Titus*, 512.
[200] Yarbrough, *Letters to Timothy and Titus*, 513.

ate family. Marriages go up and down but, in our current Christan marriage vows, husbands and wives are joined together 'for better, for worse; for richer or poorer'. This is the type of relationship of which Paul writes: a genuine commitment from wives and husbands to each other and their children.

The family is the basic building block of any sane, rational society. But today it is under fierce attack by neo-Marxists and those wishing to inflict identity politics on western society, where everyone is either classed as some type of victim or the member of a 'tribe', like 'women', 'the poor', 'conservatives', etc. Each tribe is encouraged to find resentment against another tribe(s), thus dividing society rather than finding means of uniting people under common values and purposes. The church is not immune to this social destruction when various denominations accuse one another of this or that 'heresy' and refuse to have communication (let alone communion) with the other party. The family of God in Christ ought to be an example to itself and the outside world that love (both *agapē* and *philos*) covers many sins. Given that time is shorter than when these words were written nearly 2,000 years ago, Christians must be more aware and active in union than dissension. Jesus is coming!

7 The end of all things is near; therefore, be of sound judgment and sober *spirit* for the purpose of prayer.
8 Above all, keep fervent in your love for one another, because love covers a multitude of sins.
9 Be hospitable to one another without complaint.
10 As each one has received a *special* gift, employ it in serving one another as good stewards of the manifold grace of God.
11 Whoever speaks, *is to do so* as one who is speaking the utterances of God; whoever serves *is to do so* as one who is serving by the strength which God supplies; so that in all things God may be glorified through

Jesus Christ, to whom belongs the glory and dominion forever and ever. Amen.

1 Peter 4:7-11 (emphasis added)

NASB

How much do Peter's words sound like Titus' instructions for the churches?! Love in families is the beginning of a cord that encompasses societies, especially the church gathered together. It is noteworthy that it is neither Paul nor Titus who should instruct younger women but older women, who are best placed to teach by example and personal encouragement.

2:5 in Detail

σώφρονας, ἁγνάς, οἰκουργούς,[201] ἀγαθάς, ὑποτασσομένας τοῖς ἰδίοις ἀνδράσιν, ἵνα μὴ ὁ λόγος τοῦ θεοῦ βλασφημῆται. to be sensible, pure, keepers at home, kind, being subject to their own husbands, so that the word of God will not be blasphemed.

This is the third time that Paul has used *sōphrōn* and it is clearly a critical component of genuine Christian living. To a greater or lesser extent both older and younger members of the church can possess this quality. Paul provides examples of this sensible behaviour. After being sensible, younger women should be 'pure' (ἁγνός - *agnos*). This is a quality necessary for all Christians (cf. 1 John 3:3).

201 See Bernard, *The Pastoral Epistles*, 167 re his preference for οἰκουγούς and a lengthy explanation of this word. Mounce, *Pastoral Epistles*, 405d agrees with Bernard's interpretation that the word should be οἰκουγούς, commenting, that this word 'like many of the terms in this passage, was held up as a laudable quality in a wife by secular writers. Its textual evidence is widespread, and it does fit the discussion better.'

Reflecting the social conditions in Crete in the first century, women generally worked at home and Paul regards these domestic responsibilities as important. To be busy tending one's home also reduces time for idle gossiping (2:3). Young women must be kind (ἀγαθάς - *agathas*), the kind spirit envisioned in Christian love (*agapē*). This quality can be misinterpreted as suggesting that wives should be completely housebound. The NT has plenty of examples of women who were active outside their homes, such as Lydia (Acts 16:14), Prisca (Acts 18:3), Phoebe (Rom. 16:1) and several women named in Romans 16 (cf. Prov. 31:10-31). Although begun c 610 AD, Islam, in its more fundamental practices, still subjugates women severely in terms of their dress and activities outside the home. Christianity differs substantially in this respect and treats women with dignity in all aspects of their lives. 'Nothing in the New Testament suggests that Paul (or Jesus) had a draconian intent to restrict women's public presence or movements, confining them perhaps to a harem of one.'[202]

The young women are assumed to be Christians and must be subject (ὑποτάσσω - *hupotassō*) to their own husbands, regardless of their husbands' religious position. This word is also used in 2:9 regarding slaves and their masters and in 3:1 regarding citizens and rulers). 'The adjective ἰδίοις (*idiois*) limits the submissiveness of these young women to their own husbands, not to men in general.'[203] See 1 Tim 2:8. This is now a most controversial instruction in modern Christianity. Feminism and women's rights movements have made the issue of a woman's right to determine her future a major battle in secular society. It is now a dominant theme in many churches where it is asserted by men and women that women have the right to hold any office in the church (egalitarianism). This

[202] Yarbrough, *Letters to Timothy and Titus*, 516.
[203] Perkins, *The Pastoral Letters*, 262.

position has expanded to the extent that the ordination of women has become commonplace in many protestant denominations, but not all. Reformed denominations will not submit to this practice, rather arguing that Scripture (based on the principles of Genesis 2-3), requires that the man is the head of the family with his wife complementing his leadership (complementarianism).[204] Young women are to adopt such behaviour so that the word of God will not be dishonoured. Bray provides important insights into the social and family customs of the times and how the gospel would mould them into a more Christian lifestyle.

> Paul insisted that a woman should obey her *own* husband because otherwise the word of God might be blasphemed, and the word of God made it plain that when a couple married, they were to leave father and mother and become one flesh (Gen. 2:24; Matt. 19:5; Eph. 5:31). Economic circumstances might complicate matters in practice, but the principle nevertheless had to be maintained. A daughter-in-law was not an extra daughter, and still less a slave. She was the son's wife, and it was to him, not to his father, that she was primarily responsible. Here we have an interesting example of how the gospel could subtly undermine social traditions not by removing them altogether but by substituting a higher ideal for them. ... Paul could not break up the extended family and probably did not want to, but he could establish boundaries within it that would eventually bring about a profound transformation of the way it worked. The nuclear family, as we call it today, was the desired Biblical norm, and Paul expected to see it worked out in the rather different social and economic context that he had to deal with.[205]

A further requirement is that these young women should be 'kind' (ἀγαθός – *agathos*) (NASB, NIV, RSV, ESV,

---

[204] I have argued strongly for the complementarian position in my book, *Gender Wars in Christianity*.

[205] Bray, *The Pastoral Epistles*, 511.

NEB). As Yarbrough points out, this is not the meaning of the Greek word. When referring to people, it means 'good' (cf. Joseph of Arimathea in Luke 23:50; Dorcas in Acts 9:36; and Barnabas in Acts 11:24). It may sound rather banal to seek for someone to be 'good' but, in a first century context, it meant being of exemplary virtue. That should still be the case today.

There is a constant refrain through the letter that the *gospel* must not be brought into disrepute. It is one thing to criticise the messenger but Paul cannot contemplate the person, work and message of Jesus to be a reason for any valid criticism of the Church.

2:6 in Detail

τοὺς νεωτέρους ὡσαύτως παρακάλει σωφρονεῖν·
Likewise urge the young men to be sensible;

As in 2:3, 5, Paul uses 'likewise' (ὡσαύτως - *hōsautōs*) to include the young men in displaying the characteristic of *sōphrōn*. Titus is not just to speak to the young men: he is to urge (exhort) (παρακάλει - *parakalei*) them to sensible behaviour. Paul uses the imperative of this verb to reinforce the strength of his direction to Titus. It seems clear that to be of a sound mind is one of Paul's most important principles in practical Christian living. In Romans 12:2 the apostle confronted two opposites. The ungodly would 'be conformed to this world' with its temptations and sins. The alternative for Christians is for them to 'be *transformed* by the *renewing of your mind,* so that *you may prove* what the will of God is, that which is good and acceptable and perfect' (emphases added). In modern society there are many influences at play on the minds of young men (and women!) but renewal by the Holy Spirit is only possible by 'presenting your bodies as a *living* sacrifice, acceptable to God' (Rom. 12:1). Paul reinforces that it is a person's mind which is at the heart of transformation. Those whom

God has chosen to be His people will be influenced in their minds (initially) by the Spirit, which will then spread to belief and practice. How much better for this to occur in the young than the old!

In our current society many families are dysfunctional, particularly because of the absence of a father. Elders have the opportunity to be role models for boys and younger men who need masculine examples in their lives.[206] The OT had much to say about young men and the way they should conduct themselves (cf. Prov. 20:29; Eccles. 11:9a) but warns that evil will befall the wicked (cf. 2 Kings 2:24). Therefore, it was important for the young men to grow into mature men, some of whom might become elders themselves.

> Their imitation of him [Titus] was more a matter of spiritual principle than of practical application, because most of them would have been tied to their family farms or businesses and would remain so. But that did not stop them seeking to be like Titus in their character and behaviour, and if Titus succeeded in producing young men of that stamp, he would have done more for the church in Crete than he would have achieved by preaching a thousand sermons.
>
> The reason for that is simple. People notice when lives are changed. ...
>
> Young men like a challenge, and if they are challenged to memorize the Ten Commandments instead of to break as many of them as possible at one sitting, the transformation will be electric. This is what Paul wanted to see and why he instructed in this way.[207]

---

[206] See MacArthur, *1-2 Timothy and Titus*, 228 regarding Paul's teaching method as applied to Timothy (2 Tim. 2:1-2).

[207] Bray, *The Pastoral Epistles*, 512-13. See Yarbrough, *Letters to Timothy and Titus*, 520, where 'young men are susceptible to particular blandishments and allurements that detract from godly aims. Even

Again, there is the emphasis on the characteristic of *sōphrōn.*

Titus to be an Example

2:7 *in all things show yourself to be an example of good deeds, with purity in doctrine, dignified,*
2:8 *sound in speech which is beyond reproach, so that the opponent will be put to shame, having nothing bad to say about us.*
NASB

2:7 in Detail

περὶ πάντα σεαυτὸν παρεχόμενος τύπον καλῶν ἔργων, ἐν τῇ διδασκαλίᾳ ἀφθορίαν, σεμνότητα,
in all things show yourself to be an example of good deeds, with purity in doctrine, dignified,

Paul now turns from his comments about people in the churches to Titus himself. Having told Titus what ought to be expected of elders and congregations, he now advises Titus about his own behaviour. There will be high expectations! Titus is *in all things* (περὶ πάντα – *peri panta*) to show himself as an example (παρεχόμενος τύπον – *parechomenos tupon*) of good deeds. The word τύπος (*tupos*) means the impress of a die, which is not alterable. This word might be compared with εἰκών (*eikōn*) in Colossians 1:15, which is the die used for making exact images on coins. In their translation, Zerwick and Grosvenor note that *parechomenos* is associated with good deeds (καλῶν ἔργων – *kalōn ergōn*), rather than *sōphrōn.*[208] 'Because the heathen cannot see our faith, they ought to see our works, then hear our

lawful pursuits and callings may become objects of idolatrous devotion.'

208 Zerwick and Grosvenor, *Analysis of the Greek New Testament*, vol. 2, 649.

doctrine, and then be converted.'[209] His conduct will reflect adversely on his opponents, who are 'unfit for doing anything good' (1:16). But Titus is to be an example, not only in the content, but in the manner, of his speaking and teaching. In these circumstances Titus is to be humble, recognising that all people are made in God's image. There is no room for lording it over the Cretans but, on the contrary, an uncompromising declaration of the truth of the gospel by one who was once in their position before God.

> For the Christian, status and validity do not rest upon relative relationships to other men. As a Christian I do not have to find my validity in my status, or by thinking myself above other men. My validity and my status are found in being before the God who is there. My basic validity and my basic status do not depend upon what men think of me. So the problems of superiority are set in a completely different framework, and I can deal with them without fearing that if I limit my feeling and practice of superiority my value, my validity, and status will be totally lost.[210]

Regardless of much Christian opinion to the contrary, doctrine does matter. But, perhaps, it is not just about having the correct doctrine about the fundamentals of the Christian faith. No doubt, Paul wanted Titus to ensure that correct teaching and understanding occurred, but Paul also counselled Titus in his manner of addressing these new churches. Paul describes the doctrines taught by Titus as 'pure' (ἀφθορία - *aphthoria*), which is its only use in the NT. 'It means "soundness, uncorruptness, single-mindedness".'[211] The reference to 'purity' is not to doc-

---

[209] Martin Luther, *Luther's Works*. J. Pelikan ed. (St Louis: Concordia, 1966), 29:57.

[210] F. A. Schaeffer, *Substantial Healing of the Total Person* in F. A. Schaeffer, *The Complete Works of Francis A. Schaeffer: A Christian Worldview*, 5 vols. (Wheaton, IL: Crossway, 1982), vol. 3, 333-34.

[211] Mounce, *Pastoral Epistles*, 413.

trine that teaches 'pure' morality but that which, in itself, is wholesome and completely compatible with Paul's (and Jesus') teaching. Some of us want to ensure that, when it comes to doctrine, 'every nail is hammered firmly into the fence' so that error will be dispelled. However, a comment from Bill Muhlenberg provides wisdom about the technique we might use in driving in those nails.

> But none of us are perfect, none of us have it all together, none of us have inerrant doctrine, and none of us are in a place where we should sit in judgment on everyone else around us. Yes, we discern, we evaluate lifestyles, we evaluate what a person believes, but we do so carefully and graciously.[212]

This seems consistent with Paul's two aims for Titus: tell the truth with grace. For this he will need to be dignified (σεμνότης - *semnotēs*). Other relevant meanings can be probity or honour. As he was in Corinth (cf. 2 Cor. 7:14), Titus would be an adornment to the gospel (cf. 2:10).

2:8 in Detail

λόγον ὑγιῆ ἀκατάγνωστον, ἵνα ὁ ἐξ ἐναντίας ἐντραπῇ μηδὲν ἔχων λέγειν περὶ ἡμῶν φαῦλον.
sound in speech which is beyond reproach, so that the opponent will be put to shame, having nothing bad to say about us.

As noted in the previous verse, Titus would speak the truth with grace (and courage). His primarily Jewish opponents (1:10-14) will not only be embarrassed by the faithful gospel message but also be put to shame by having nothing derogatory to say about either Titus the man or his message. 'φαῦλος [*phaulos*: 'bad' or 'evil'] is in the

---

[212] W. Muehlenberg, *Evangelical Pharisees and the God We Serve*. See 'CultureWatch' at *www.billmuehlenberg.com*, 7 May 2024.

NT always applied to evil deeds rather than evil words; and so the point of this clause is that the opponents of St Paul's 'sound doctrine' have nothing scandalous to report of his conduct or of that of Titus.'[213] (cf. John 3:20; Jas. 3:16).

Instructions on Behaviour of Slaves

2:9 *Urge bondslaves to be subject to their own masters in everything, to be well-pleasing, not argumentative,*
2:10 *not pilfering, but showing all good faith so that they will adorn the doctrine of God our Saviour in every respect.* NASB

2:9 in Detail

δούλους ἰδίοις δεσπόταις ὑποτάσσεσθαι ἐν πᾶσιν, εὐαρέστους εἶναι, μὴ ἀντιλέγοντας,
Urge slaves to be subject to their own masters in everything, to be well-pleasing, not obstinant,

Slavery was common throughout the Roman Empire in the first century AD, as was discussed in 1:1 above. Given that Paul is addressing Titus in a Christian context, we should only see his instruction as applying to slaves (male and female) who were Christians. Unlike Colossians 4:11, Paul has nothing to say to the masters of slaves.[214] Paul enjoins slaves to 'obey' (ὑπακούω – *hupakouō*) their masters in Ephesians 6:5 and Colossians 3:22-23 but, here, he requires slaves to 'submit' [be subject to] their masters. 'The latter word is rather the stronger, perhaps suggesting a greater tendency on the part of Christian slaves in Crete to abuse their new-found emancipation in Christ.'[215]

---

[213] Bernard, *The Pastoral Epistles*, 169.

[214] It seems to me highly improbable to assume that every Christian slave was owned by a Christian master. See Mounce, *Pastoral Epistles*, 415.

[215] Guthrie, *The Pastoral Epistles*, 196.

Paul's attitude to the Christian requirements for slaves is his use of εὐαρέστος (*euarestos*) to describe the way they should please their masters. Slaves should be more cognisant of their status as Christians, rather than as slaves. In each other use of the word Paul applies it to the pleasing of God or Christ (cf. Rom.12:1, 2; 14:18; 2 Cor. 5:9; Eph. 5:10; Phlp. 4:18; Col. 3:20; also Heb. 13:21.)

Even slaves should not bring the gospel into disrepute. On the contrary, the willing obedience of slaves could very well influence the disposition of their masters.[216] Some slaves would have worked in household duties where their demeanour and pleasing (εὐαρέστος - *euarestos*) attitude would have differentiated them from other slaves. While they are urged to be obedient to their masters 'in everything', Paul and Titus would not expect them to be submissive to directions contrary to Christian beliefs.[217] The words μὴ ἀντιλέγοντας (*mē antilegontas*) mean much more than just arguing with words. They reflect a much deeper opposition to their instructions (see its use in 1:9).

2:10 in Detail

μὴ νοσφιζομένους, ἀλλὰ πᾶσαν πίστιν ἐνδεικνυμένους ἀγαθήν, ἵνα τὴν διδασκαλίαν τὴν τοῦ σωτῆρος ἡμῶν θεοῦ κοσμῶσιν ἐν πᾶσιν.
not pilfering but showing all good faith so that they will adorn the doctrine of God our Saviour in every respect.

The intensity of Paul's instructions may be reflected in the prevalence of slaves throughout the Roman Empire (who owned, and were entitled to, nothing) to engage in petty theft (νοσφιζομένους - *nosphizomenous*) from their masters. The word's use in Acts 5:2-3 to describe the

[216] See Yarbrough, *Letters to Timothy and Titus*, 524.
[217] See Guthrie, *The Pastoral Epistles*, 196.

fraudulence of Ananias and Sapphira means that it can describe more serious crime. On the contrary, slaves were to demonstrate proof (ἐνδείκνυμι - *endeiknumi*) that they were faithful in all things (cf. 1 Tim. 6:1-2). By doing this, they will adorn the gospel in every respect. κοσμῶσιν (*kosmōsin*) was the word used to describe the setting of a jewel 'and so, here, "the doctrine of God our Saviour" is, as it were, "set off", and exhibited in a favourable light to the unbelieving world, by the conduct of those who, *in whatever station*, profess belief in it.'[218]

With this instruction we see the new society that the Christian gospel was developing. Paul is not writing to lords and masters: he is writing to slaves, the least valued of all people in that society. Yet he uses royal language to describe their position in Christ's family. They are considered sufficiently worthy as to be able to please their masters as they would Christ himself. They are described like precious stones (cf. 1 Pet. 1:6-7). While Paul (and Jesus) accepted the reality of slavery, they prescribed ways for the oppressed to find dignity in their work as sons and daughters of the living God. This was the subtle influence that was turning the world upside down (Acts 16:20), albeit very slowly in the case of slavery.

The Outcome of Salvation

2:11 *For the grace of God has appeared, bringing salvation to all men,*

2:12 *instructing us to deny ungodliness and worldly desires and to live sensibly, righteously and godly in the present age,*

2:13 *looking for the blessed hope and the appearing of the glory of our great God and Saviour, Christ Jesus,*

---

[218] Bernard, *The Pastoral Epistles*, 170 (emphasis added).

2:14 *who gave Himself for us to redeem us from every lawless deed, and to purify for Himself a people for His own possession, zealous for good deeds.*
2:15 *These things speak and exhort and reprove with all authority. Let no one disregard you.*
NASB

2:11 in Detail

ἐπεφάνη γὰρ ἡ χάρις τοῦ θεοῦ σωτήριος πᾶσιν ἀνθρώποις, For the grace of God has appeared, bringing salvation to all men,

Verses 11-14 contain an important doctrinal statement from Paul. It is the theological basis for the practical instructions he has given to Titus in 1:1-9; 2:1-10. Mounce notes that 'many of the terms and ideas are deeply rooted in the OT and Paul's own thought, and in firm contrast to the Hellenistic ideal of education resulting in virtue; the virtuous Christian life is firmly grounded in the redemptive work of Christ.'[219] Paul's use of the verb 'to appear' (ἐπιφαίνειν – *epiphainein*) is important, especially for the Jews in the churches. This word is used in the LXX to describe the appearing of God's face (Num. 6:25; Ps. 30:17; 66:2; 79:4, 8, 20; 117:27; 118:135). Of course, for Christians, the appearing of God's face on earth occurred during the lifetime of Jesus, as declared in John 1:14: 'And *the Word became flesh*, and dwelt among us, and we saw His glory, glory as of the only begotten from the Father, *full of grace and truth*' (emphasis added). However, the emphasis here is not on who appeared but what appeared: the grace of God.

'For' (γὰρ – gar) explains why all the Christians on Crete should behave in the manner explained by Titus. It is because the grace of God has appeared, which

[219] Mounce, *Pastoral Epistles*, 421.

(through the Holy Spirit) teaches men and women, Jew and Gentile, young and old, slave and free, how to please God and adorn the gospel by their right living, personally and with each other. This grace from God also brings salvation (eternal life) to those who hear and believe the gospel of Christ. As Paul writes in 1:3, grace appeared to the Cretans by his (and Titus') preaching of the gospel which was entrusted to Paul 'by the commandment of God our Saviour' (see comments on 1:3). Belief in the gospel delivers people from sin and God's condemnation. Paul announces that salvation has not only appeared to the Cretans but to all men (πᾶσιν ἀνθρώποις – *pasin anthrōpois*), but it will only have salvific effect on *those whom God has chosen*.

2:12 in Detail

παιδεύουσα ἡμᾶς ἵνα ἀρνησάμενοι τὴν ἀσέβειαν καὶ τὰς κοσμικὰς ἐπιθυμίας σωφρόνως καὶ δικαίως καὶ εὐσεβῶς ζήσωμεν ἐν τῷ νῦν αἰῶνι,
instructing us to deny ungodliness and worldly desires and to live sensibly, righteously and godly in the present age,

Through grace, the gospel not only 'instructs' but also trains and disciplines the believer about right and wrong, good and bad. It is as if grace acts as a teacher. Yarbrough notes that 'grace is extended *so that humans might extend themselves* to lay hold of it. … Only robust pursuit of grace appropriates it.'[220] Negatively, it teaches the avoidance and *renunciation* of 'ungodliness and worldly desires' (τὴν ἀσέβειαν καὶ τὰς κοσμικὰς ἐπιθυμίας – *tēn asebeian kai tas kosmikas epithumias*). In Romans 1:18 ungodliness is a primary reason for the exercise of God's wrath. 'Worldly' desires come from Satan (cf. Matt. 4:8 concerning Satan's tempta-

[220] Yarbrough, *Letters to Timothy and Titus*, 528 (emphasis added).

tion of Jesus; John 15:18-19). The 'world' (κόςμος - *kosmos*) refers to life on earth and its pursuits and pleasures (cf. 1 Cor. 2:12; 3:19). 'The three-termination adjective κοσμικός occurs only once in the Pastoral Epistles but is also found in Hebrews 9:1, where it describes the "earthly sanctuary," i.e., the tabernacle. It characterises something as pertaining to the κόςμος which in contrast to the heavenly realm may have connotations of inferior moral or other status.'[221] Although we are *in* the world, we are not to be *of* the world (cf. Rom. 12:2). It is not good enough just to say that certain things or practises are wrong. We must go further. 'Chrystostom comments, "See here the foundation of all virtue. He [Paul] has not said 'avoiding,' but 'denying.' Denying implies the greatest difference, the greatest hatred and aversion" ("Homily 5"; NPNF 13:536).'[222] Grace helps us to have nothing to do with ungodliness.

The positive emphasis of grace is that people should live with self-control (note the emphasis again on *sōphrōn*), righteously and in a godly manner. All the requirements for such a life have already been covered by Paul in the verses above. Living 'righteously' could be translated living 'justly' (δικαίως - *dikaiōs*), the word that speaks of justification (cf. Rom. 3:24). Their living should reflect their justified status through Christ's redemptive work. That the Cretans need to lead 'godly' lives is a constant theme in this letter. This verse speaks about the present time (νῦν αἰῶνι - *nun aiōni*) when Paul is writing to Titus. It applies equally to us in the twenty-first century: *this* present age. God hasn't changed his mind. What was written then is for our instruction now.

---

221 Perkins, *The Pastoral Letters*, 268.

222 Mounce, *Pastoral Epistles*, 424.

2:13 in Detail

προσδεχόμενοι τὴν μακαρίαν ἐλπίδα καὶ ἐπιφάνειαν τῆς δόξης τοῦ μεγάλου θεοῦ καὶ σωτῆρος ἡμῶν ἰησοῦ χριστοῦ, awaiting the blessed hope and the appearing of the glory of our great God and Saviour, Jesus Christ,

Christians are to 'await'[223] the appearing of Christ. As with Paul's letter to the Thessalonians (2 Thess. 2:6), the appearing of Christ is a certainty, although its timing is unknown. 'Waiting' is a distinctly Jewish and Christian experience, emphasised in both the OT and NT regarding God and His word (cf. Gen. 49:18; Ps. 25:5; 27:14; 119:114, 147; Luke 2:25; Rom. 8:25; 1 Cor. 4:5; Phlp. 3:20 NASB). 'Hope' is described in the *Compact Oxford English Dictionary* as 'a *feeling* of expectation and *desire* for something to happen' (emphasis added). Nothing could be further from the concept of Christian hope: 'To hope means *to look forward expectantly for God's future activity*. The ground of hope is God's past activity in Jesus Christ, who points the way to God's purposes for his creation' (emphasis added).'[224] Christian hope does not refer to expectations or feelings but looks forward to events (what is hoped for).

These Christians are to look forward with certainty to the return of Jesus in glory. He is described as both God (the Creator) and Saviour (the Redeemer). Titus is to inform these Cretan Christians that the return of Christ is a wonderful incentive to live in a way that pleases him because its occurrence could be at any time.

The use of και between ἐλπίδα and ἐπιφάνειαν τῆς δόξης is not just as a joining word used between two related concepts. Perkins notes that και is used appositionally; i.e. the appearing of 'the glory of our great God and

---

[223] 'Wait for an event': *Compact Oxford English Dictionary*, 59.

[224] Travis, *Hope* in *New Dictionary of Theology*, 321.

Saviour' is placed next to 'hope' so that the latter concept explains the former.[225]

Paul's reference to 'the great God' (τοῦ μεγάλου θεοῦ – *tou megalou Theou*) is unique in the NT but is a frequent description in the LXX (cf. Deut. 10:17; Neh. 8:6; Isa. 26:4; Dan. 2:45). The Granville Sharp rule[226] means that both 'God' and 'Saviour' refer to Jesus. However, this phrase in 2:13 is open to several interpretations but I favour the use of the Granville Sharp rule.[227] Jesus is divine (i.e. God,

---

225 See Perkins, *The Pastoral Letters*, 269.

226 The terms 'God' and 'Saviour' both refer to the same person. The construction in Greek is known as the Granville Sharp rule, named after the English philanthropist-linguist who first clearly articulated the rule in 1798. Sharp pointed out that in the construction 'article-noun-καί-noun' (where καί [*kai*] = 'and'), when two nouns are singular, personal, and common (i.e., not proper names), they *always* had the same referent. Illustrations such as 'the friend and brother', 'the God and Father', etc. abound in the NT to prove Sharp's point; e.g. Jude 4; 2 Pet. 1:1.

Granville Sharp (1735–1813) was an English political reformer, slavery abolitionist, and Greek language scholar known for his contributions regarding the translation of New Testament Greek as it relates to the divinity of Christ. Sharp believed strongly in the deity of Christ and studied the New Testament in its original language to more ably prove Christ's deity. The Granville Sharp rule was first noted in 1798 in his book, *Remarks on the Uses of the Definitive Article in the Greek Text of the New Testament: Containing Many New Proofs of the Divinity of Christ, from Passages Which Are Wrongly Translated in the Common English Version.*

The Granville Sharp rule states, 'When the copulative *kai* connects two nouns of the same case, [viz. nouns (either substantive or adjective, or participles) of personal description, respecting office, dignity, affinity, or connexion, and attributes, properties, or qualities, good or ill], if the article *ho*, or any of its cases, precedes the first of the said nouns or participles, and is not repeated before the second noun or participle, the latter always relates to the same person that is expressed or described by the first noun or participle.' (*Remarks on the Uses of the Definitive Article*, 3).

See *https://www.gotquestions.org/Granville-Sharp-Rule.html* (accessed 8 November 2024).

227 See Mounce, *Pastoral Epistles*, 426-31 for a comprehensive analysis of different interpretations of θεὸς καὶ σωτήρ. Kelly's commentary on

although he is the Son, he is not the Father) and he is also Saviour. It is the appearing of Jesus Christ (the great God and Saviour) in glory that is our blessed hope (cf. 3:4).

> The use of 'great' is better explained if it refers to Christ. Nowhere else in the NT is the adjective 'great' used of God. Bernard, 172, holds that there must be some special reason for using this unique term here, that it is somewhat pointless if applied to God [the Father], but it is significant if applied to Christ, whose epiphany is awaited. Harris argues that the adjective is fitly used of Jesus as 'God and Saviour' and that it is then explained in v 14. More convincing is Houlden's suggestion that the writer is contrasting 'our deity' with the pagan divinities of surrounding peoples.[228]

2:14 in Detail

ὃς ἔδωκεν ἑαυτὸν ὑπὲρ ἡμῶν ἵνα λυτρώσηται ἡμᾶς ἀπὸ πάσης ἀνομίας καὶ καθαρίσῃ ἑαυτῷ λαὸν περιούσιον, ζηλωτὴν καλῶν ἔργων.

who gave Himself for us to redeem us from every lawless deed, and to purify for Himself a people for His own possession, zealous for good deeds.

Jesus is not only Saviour, but Redeemer. Hence Paul's use of the verb λυτρόω (*lutroō*): to redeem. Jesus himself described His role as giving His life as a 'ransom (λύτρον - *lutron*) for many' (Matt. 20:28; Mark 10:45; cf. Heb. 9:12). The practice of ransom was widespread across the Roman Empire because pirates would kidnap wealthy

---

this verse translates τοῦ μεγάλου θεοῦ καὶ σωτῆρος ἡμῶν ἰησοῦ χριστοῦ as 'the great God and our Saviour Christ Jesus' (p 246). I have some concern about his claim 'that Paul nowhere else, either in these or his other letters, explicitly describes Christ as God (Rom. 9:5 may be an exception) (p 247).' This ignores Trinitarian passages such as Col. 1:15-17; Heb. 1:3, where Christ and God are identified together.

[228] Marshall with Towner, *The Pastoral Epistles*, 280.

people and hold them for ransom. When the ransom was paid, the captive was set free. Jesus paid the ransom price for our lives to be free completely.[229] Jesus did this not only for us, but for His own benefit so that he could have a purified people for *his own* possession (ἑαυτῷ λαὸν περιούσιον - *eautō laon periousion*). The OT often refers to God's people as being His special possession. The Greek word περιούσιος (*periousios*) is a NT *hapax* and is the LXX translation of a Hebrew word that signifies a 'treasured possession' (Ex. 19:5; Deut. 7:6; 14:2; 26:18 NIV).

> The stress in the verse lies on this purpose clause [ἵνα λυτρώσηται ἡμᾶς ἀπὸ πάσης ἀνομίας - *hina lutrōsētai hēmas apo pasēs anomias*] which expresses the effects of Christ's self-giving. It has two balanced parts. On the one hand, Christ has redeemed his people from all evil. On the other hand, he has created a new people, i.e. a new Israel, who will do good works. Both actions are antitypical of the actions of Yahweh. At the Exodus he delivered the Israelites from slavery and made them his own people. Already in the OT the concept of redemption is spiritualised to refer to deliverance from sin. Thus Christ here has the same roles as Yahweh: the 'high' Christology of v 13 is maintained. The Christian church is described as his 'Israel'. To the negative deliverance from evil corresponds the positive zeal for doing good.[230]

This was the cost of our justification before God by which he 'is faithful and righteous to forgive us our sins and to cleanse us from all unrighteousness' (1 John 1:9; cf. Ezek. 37:23b). The need for purity in thought and behaviour is a constant biblical theme but cleansing comes from God (cf. Eph. 5:26). It goes without saying that such a special people should strive vigorously to do

---

[229] The concept of Christ's ransom for sinners was fully developed in L. L. Morris, *The Apostolic Preaching of the Cross* (Leicester: Inter-Varsity Press, 1965).

[230] Marshall with Towner, *The Pastoral Epistles*, 283-84.

good works to honour their master. ζηλωτὴν (*zēlōtēn*) is a standard Jewish term employed to describe a person who is a Yahweh loyalist (e.g., 2 Macc. 4:2). It is also used in earlier Greek literature to describe someone committed to specific ideas or ideals. In this case, it is to be zealous for the gospel.

> Paul envisions not a dogged acceptance of religious commandments but a real zeal. 'A people … eager to do what is good' could be rendered literally 'a zealot people when it comes to good works.' While religious fervour can be misguided and dangerous, its absence is no less ominous. Paul praised it among fellow Jews (Rom. 10:2a), and Jesus expressed disgust for its lack: he will spew the lukewarm Laodiceans out of his mouth (Rev. 3:16). A hostile social environment like Crete can tempt the church to lie low, nurse its grievances, and turn inward. Paul calls for renewed attention to Jesus's death as a reminder that, in God's economy, the grain of wheat that dies yields an abundant harvest (see John 12:24). That harvest takes the form of lives actively fulfilling and surpassing God's commands and leading.[231]

In our current society, where Christianity is despised more than it is respected, this is a serious warning for the church not to hide away, not to be afraid of declaring gospel truth, not to be ashamed of Jesus, but to combat evil by the power of the Spirit.

2:15 in Detail

ταῦτα λάλει καὶ παρακάλει καὶ ἔλεγχε μετὰ πάσης ἐπιταγῆς· μηδείς σου περιφρονείτω.
These things speak and exhort and reprove with all authority. Let no one disregard you.

[231] Yarbrough, *Letters to Timothy and Titus*, 532.

This instruction is for Titus himself because the elders are yet to be chosen. The multiple verbs stress both the positive ('speak' and 'exhort') and the negative ('reprove with all authority') aspects of Titus' role with the Cretan churches regarding 2:1-14. 'The basic meaning of ἐλέγχω is "bring to light, expose, set forth." On the use of ἐλέγχω in the Pastoral Epistles, see 1 Tim 5:20.'[232] If Titus needs to rebuke bad behaviour or doctrine, he should do so 'with all authority'. As Paul's delegate on Crete Titus has apostolic authority to denounce what is, and who are, wrong. Titus will not only exhort the Cretans to adopt Christian beliefs and practices but also bring to light wrong behaviour and ideas. There is a final comment from Paul to encourage Titus: μηδείς σου περιφρονείτω (*mēdeis sou periphroneitō*) 'Let no one look down on [disregard] you' (cf. 1 Tim. 4:12). This phrase can be translated as strongly as: 'let no one have contempt for you'. 'Why would Paul express concern for Titus? Perhaps because there was a natural opposition to authority, especially when that authority was demanding a change in behaviour. Anyone in Titus' position, even Paul, would have been looked upon with disdain, especially considering Cretan culture.'[233]

> The entire thrust of vv 11-15 is that the Christian ethic stems not from what this present age teaches but from the revolutionary work of the redeeming God who has brought salvation by his mercy and grace (3:3-7), and it is conditioned by eschatological expectations. In the PE [Pastoral Epistles] God's grace is the instructor, not Hellenistic philosophy.[234]

[232] Perkins, *The Pastoral Letters*, 272.
[233] Mounce, *Pastoral Epistles*, 433.
[234] Mounce, *Pastoral Epistles*, 425.

CHAPTER 3

An Ongoing Emphasis on Godly Behaviour

3:1 *Remind them to be subject to rulers, to authorities, to be*
obedient, to be ready for every good deed,
3:2 *to malign no one, to be peaceable, gentle, showing every*
consideration for all men.
3:3 *For we also once were foolish ourselves, disobedient,*
deceived, enslaved to various lusts and pleasures, spending
our life in malice and envy, hateful, hating one another.
3:4 *But when the kindness of God our Savior and His love for*
mankind appeared,
3:5 *He saved us, not on the basis of deeds which we have done*
in righteousness, but according to His mercy, by the wash-
ing of regeneration and renewing by the Holy Spirit,
3:6 *whom He poured out upon us richly through Jesus Christ*
our Savior,
3:7 *so that being justified by His grace we would be made heirs*
according to the hope of eternal life.
3:8 *This is a trustworthy statement; and concerning these*
things I want you to speak confidently, so that those who
have believed God will be careful to engage in good deeds.
These things are good and profitable for men.

3:9 *But avoid foolish controversies and genealogies and strife and disputes about the Law, for they are unprofitable and worthless.*
3:10 *Reject a factious man after a first and second warning,*
3:11 *knowing that such a man is perverted and is sinning, being self-condemned.*
NASB

Chapter 3:1-11 is similar to 2:1-14 in that these verses describe God's plan for salvation and the type of behaviour that will be displayed by his people. In this section, Titus is to provide the Christians with justification for his call that believers have a gracious attitude to all people. This theological basis encourages believers to do good works and avoid pointless arguments. Those who will not cooperate will be disciplined.

3:1 in Detail

ὑπομίμνῃσκε αὐτοὺς ἀρχαῖς ἐξουσίαις ὑποτάσσεσθαι, πειθαρχεῖν, πρὸς πᾶν ἔργον ἀγαθὸν ἑτοίμους εἶναι,
Remind them to be subject to rulers, to authorities, to be obedient, to be ready for every good deed,

Notwithstanding any contempt or disapproval that he receives, Titus is to press on with his godly lifestyle, teaching the pure gospel and speaking to repel any opposition to his message in the Cretan churches. In this verse Paul continues to exhort Titus by calling on him to remind 'them': i.e. all the Cretan Christians of their duties as citizens. 'Remind' is in the present tense, with the implication of '*keep on reminding* them'. The proper role of the state (rulers and authorities: ἄρχοντες (*archontes*) [καὶ] ἐξουσίας (*exousias*)) is summarised by Paul in Romans 13:1-7.

1 Every person is to be in subjection to the governing authorities. For there is no authority except from God, and those which exist are established by God.
2 whoever resists authority has opposed the ordinance of God; and they who have opposed will receive condemnation upon themselves.
3 For rulers are not a cause of fear for good behaviour, but for evil. Do you want to have no fear of authority? Do what is good and you will have praise from the same;
4 for it is a minister of God to you for good. But if you do what is evil, be afraid; for it does not bear the sword for nothing; for it is a minister of God, an avenger who brings wrath on the one who practices evil.
5 Therefore it is necessary to be in subjection, not only because of wrath, but also for conscience' sake.
6 For because of this you also pay taxes, for *rulers* are servants of God, devoting themselves to this very thing.
7 Render to all what is due them: tax to whom tax *is due*; custom to whom custom; fear to whom fear; honour to whom honour.
NASB

From his long association with Paul, Titus would have been well aware of this precept from a Christian perspective. It must be noted that there are occasions when obedience to God trumps obedience to the state. Christian history has a multitude of examples where faithful obedience subjected believers to harsh penalties (even death) under then existing laws. We are familiar with examples of the persecuted and martyrs in the twentieth century such as Corrie ten Boom, Dietrich Bonhoeffer and Wang Zhiming. Hundreds of years before there was John Bunyan. The OT mentions the midwives of Exodus 1:17; Shadrach, Meshach and Abednego in Daniel 3; Daniel himself in Daniel 6. In the NT there was Stephen (Acts 7:57-60) and Paul himself. Unless circumstances demand otherwise, Paul's advice to Titus is correct: citizens should obey the governing authorities.

Given the general Cretan culture to ignore or resist legal prescriptions, this aspect of Christian behaviour needed to be reinforced, perhaps especially for slaves (v 5). The context suggests that 'obedience' refers to the ruling authorities; however, the 'good deeds' probably has a wider reference than just civic duties, as suggested by some commentators.[235] This verse not only warns against bad behaviour but also emphasises the positive aspect of being ready to do good deeds. The Greek for 'ready' (ἕτοιμος - *hetoimos*) indicates an immediate preparedness to act (cf. Matt. 22:4; Acts 23:21; 1 Pet. 3:15). Christians must be able to act (doing good deeds) at a moment's notice. The use of the present tense for this verb in Greek shows that it is to be an ongoing virtue.

3:2 in Detail

μηδένα βλασφημεῖν, ἀμάχους εἶναι, ἐπιεικεῖς, πᾶσαν ἐνδεικνυμένους πραΰτητα πρὸς πάντας ἀνθρώπους.
to malign no one, to be peaceable, gentle, showing every consideration for all men.

Usually, blasphemy is directed at God or the gospel but, in this instance, it concerns humans. This is a reminder that believers should avoid causing offence to non-believers. Paul moves quickly back and forth from positive to negative and back again. Just as Titus is instructed to speak wisely (2:1), so all the Christians must use their tongues wisely. James' warning below applied to the Cretans and, just as surely, applies to all readers now.

[235] See W. Hendriksen, *Commentary on I and II Timothy and Titus* (London: Banner of Truth, 1959), 386.

5 So also the tongue is a small part of the body, and *yet* it boasts of great things. See how great a forest is set aflame by such a small fire!
6 And the tongue is a fire, the *very* world of iniquity; the tongue is set among our members as that which defiles the entire body, and sets on fire the course of *our* life, and is set on fire by hell.
7 For every species of beasts and birds, of reptiles and creatures of the sea, is tamed and has been tamed by the human race.
8 But no one can tame the tongue; *it is* a restless evil *and* full of deadly poison.
9 With it we bless *our* Lord and Father, and with it we curse men, who have been made in the likeness of God;
10 from the same mouth come *both* blessing and cursing.
James 3:5-10 NASB

From the Greek verb βλασφημεω (*blasphēmeō*), we derive the English word 'blaspheme', which, in this context should be translated 'slander' or 'defame'. Here it is a command to not malign a person's character. Clearly, Paul wants none of this. But this does not contradict Paul's requirement for Titus to admonish the Cretans who were wrong in deed and/or speech. The parameters of 2:1, 7 provide guidelines for the manner of Titus' speech (cf. Jesus' instructions in Matt. 18:15-17). Nor should it deter Christians from speaking the truth in strong language, even if it truthfully concerns a person's character.

So Paul moves to opposite traits such as peacefulness (ἄμαχος - *amachos*) and gentility (ἐπιεικής - *epieikēs*). 'Paul is calling for behaviour free of arrogance and proud cockiness, not a gentleness that is always deferential to everyone, a grotesque disposition that would define the Christian as a quailing caricature.'[236] He repeats the word

[236] Yarbrough, *Letters to Timothy and Titus*, 540.

ἐνδεικνυμένους (*endeiknumenous*), which he used in 2:10 concerning slaves, to emphasise that Christians must *display* a humble and gentle nature (πραΰτης - *prautēs*) to everyone (cf. 1 Cor. 4:21; Jas. 3:13; 1 Pet. 3:15), reflected by patience.

3:3 in Detail

ἦμεν γάρ ποτε καὶ ἡμεῖς ἀνόητοι,
For we also once were foolish ourselves,

Mounce has helpfully compared the texts of 2 Timothy 1:9; Titus 2:11-15; 3:3-7 in the following table.[237] 'These passages discuss why God saves believers, the appearance of Christ, what he did, how he did it, its practical implications, and its eschatological consequences. All three passages are highly Christological, especially in their use of σωτήρ, "saviour".'[238]

Titus 2:11-15	*Titus 3:3-7*	*2 Timothy 1:9*
	We were evil people.	Not because of our works but his purpose and grace.
Grace of God.	Not because of our acts of righteousness.	
Appeared.	Goodness and philanthropy of God.	
Salvation of all people.	According to his mercy. Justified by his grace.	Now visible through the appearing of our saviour Christ Jesus.
	Appeared.	

[237] Mounce, *Pastoral Epistles*, 436-37.
[238] Mounce, *Pastoral Epistles*, 436.

Training us to live godly lives.	He saved us.	Who saved us and called us with a holy calling.
Who [i .e. Christ] gave himself to redeem us from iniquity and prepare a people, a zealot for good works.	Through regeneration and renewal. Through the Holy Spirit given through Jesus Christ.vv 1-2, 9-11	Given to us in Christ. Timothy is not to be ashamed. Paul was appointed an apostle.
As we wait for the blessed hope, the appearing of the glory of our great God and saviour Jesus Christ.	God our saviour (v 4) Jesus Christ our saviour.	Our saviour Christ Jesus.
	We have an inheritance according to the hope of eternal life.	Christ abolished death and brought life and immortality through the gospel.

Once again, Paul uses γάρ (gar – *for*) as a reason for his exhortation to do good. In this verse Paul returns to the normality of the nature of all human beings. '*For* even though they knew God, they did not honour Him as God or give thanks, but they became futile in their speculations, and their foolish heart was darkened' (Rom. 1:21). The 'they/their' of Romans 1:21 refers to *every human being*; however, Greenlee suggests that 3:3 could refer only to all Christians everywhere, who *were* once foolish and disobedient and are *now* redeemed and justified.[239] Paul concedes that he was once foolish (ἀνόητος – *anontos*) until his Damascus road experience (cf. Luke 24:25; Gal. 3:1, 3). The contrast is between what the Cretans once were

[239] Greenlee, *Titus and Philemon*, 79.

(ποτε – *pote*) and what they are now. Paul is not condemning anyone in particular but *stating the fact of the universal human ignorance about God until grace provides salvation to a person.* This foolishness is a state of not understanding spiritual matters.[240] The following descriptions are 'an accurate picture of the world as seen through God's eyes and those of the redeemed.'[241] The following sins are not necessarily attributable to all Cretans but reflect the general rebellion of humanity against God's laws for living harmoniously with one another. Most correspond to the errors committed in Genesis 3-4, which have adversely affected humanity to the present time. An analysis of the similarity between the incidents of the Fall and Titus' situation are provided below. This shows that, after Adam's sin, everyone is 'infected' by sin from birth. Sin is like a spiritual DNA. Every person is born with their own DNA genome. In the same way, since the Fall, every person is born with sin in their life (cf. Ps. 51:5).

ἀπειθεῖς,
disobedient,

The circumstances involved in the Fall of Adam and Eve correspond starkly to what Paul is describing here and are displayed in the following words. Here it means rebellion against God.[242] Adam and Eve *disobeyed* God's commandment to not eat of the fruit of the tree of the knowledge of good and evil (Gen. 3:1-6). This rebellion has been passed on to everyone since that initial sin, which is part of being human. In 1:16 and 2 Timothy 3:2 this word specifically refers to children's disobedience to parents.

πλανώμενοι,

---

[240] See Greenlee, *Titus and Philemon,* 80.
[241] Mounce, *Pastoral Epistles,* 446.
[242] Zerwick and Grosvenor, *Analysis of the Greek New Testament,* vol. 2, 650.

deceived,

Eve was *deceived* by the serpent (Satan) and led astray from God's plan for them (Gen. 3:13). So humanity is continually deceived by the prince of this world (cf. John 12:31). When people have faith in Christ, the Truth (John 1:17; 14:6) displaces deception.

δουλεύοντες ἐπιθυμίαις καὶ ἡδοναῖς ποικίλαις,
enslaved to various lusts and pleasures,

Eve *lusted* after the fruit because 'the tree was good for food, and that it was a delight to the eyes, and that the tree was desirable to make *one* wise' (Gen. 3:6). *Deception* by Satan enslaves (δουλεύω - *douleuō*) people to sin and rebellion against God. There is no escape for those captured by it. Slavery to evil was a common idea in the pagan Greco-Roman world of the time. Slavery to lusts, pleasures and sexual desires were particularly condemned by the Stoics. The word 'various' (ποικίλαις - *poikilais*) applies to both types of sin. In the NT both lusts (ἐπιθυμία - *epithumia*) and pleasures (ἡδονή - *hēdonē*) always have a negative context. Their enslavement of people speaks of the tentacles of these worldly desires that entrap the foolish and deceived.

> καὶ links ἐπιθυμίαις and ἡδοναῖς, both of which have negative connotations in this passage. Spicq (1969, 2:650) notes that these two nouns in Stoicism define cardinal faults. They also occur together in Jas. 4:1-2.[243]

ἐν κακίᾳ καὶ φθόνῳ διάγοντες,
spending our life in malice and envy,

This phrase has a sense of continuity; i.e. that we were passing our time in wickedness and badness (perhaps relating more to evil thoughts) (κακίᾳ - *kakia*) and envy

[243] Perkins, *The Pastoral Letters*, 276.

(covetousness: cf. Jas. 4:1-2). This latter *invisible* sin of coveting is the beginning of all other sin. That was the initial problem faced by Eve in the Garden.

> The climax of the Ten Commandments is the tenth commandment in Exodus 20:17 – 'Thou shalt not covet thy neighbour's house; thou shalt not covet thy neighbour's wife; nor his manservant, nor his maidservant, nor his ox, nor his ass, nor anything that is thy neighbour's.' The commandment not to covet is an entirely inward thing. Coveting is never an outward thing from the very nature of the case. Actually, we break this last commandment, not to covet, before we break any of the others. Any time that we break one of the other commandments of God, it means that we have already broken this commandment, in coveting. It also means that any time we break one of the others, we break this last commandment as well. So no matter which of the other Ten Commandments you break, you break two: the commandment itself and the commandment not to covet. This is the hub of the wheel.[244]

This predicament is worse than an occasional sin. These people 'spend their lives' in malice and envy and are as endangered as those in the previous phrase.

στυγητοί, μισοῦντες ἀλλήλους.
hated, hating one another.

This phrase again takes us back to the Garden of Eden. The first demonstration of *hate* led to the murder of Cain by Abel (Gen. 4:6-8). Although not obviously referred to, the fall of humanity in the Garden of Eden has a direct linkage to what Paul wrote to Titus in this chapter *and to our present time*. Paul uses two different Greek words in his analysis. στυγητός (*stugētos* – hateful) is a NT *hapax*.

[244] F. A. Schaeffer, *The Law and the Law of Love* in F. A. Schaeffer, *The Complete Works of Francis A. Schaeffer: A Christian Worldview*, 5 vols. (Wheaton, IL: Crossway, 1982), vol. 3, 203.

> This is the only occurrence of this verb [μιςέω] in the Pastoral Epistles. Since this participle expresses an active sense (i.e., 'hating'), the preceding στυγητός probably has a passive sense (i.e., 'hated, abhorred') to avoid tautology.[245]

3:4 in Detail

ὅτε δὲ ἡ χρηστότης καὶ ἡ φιλανθρωπία ἐπεφάνη τοῦ σωτῆρος ἡμῶν θεοῦ,
But when the kindness of God our Saviour and His love for mankind appeared,

BUT. The inclusion of δὲ (*de*) is critical to the situation in which humanity finds itself in the light of 3:3. It is now clear (if it wasn't before) that every person stands guilty of sin before a holy and just God, who must demonstrate his hatred of sin. *BUT* the kindness and love of God appeared (cf. Rom.5:8; Eph. 2:3-5). The use of ὅτε (*hote*), 'when', at the beginning of this verse contrasts with (ποτε - *pote*), 'once', in the previous verse.

The use of ἡ (*hē - the*) emphasises the specific actions of God and Christ. When *the* kindness/goodness (ἡ χρηστότης - *hē chrēstotēs*) and *the* philanthropy (ἡ φιλανθρωπία - *hē philanthrōpia*) of God appeared, he saved us. This appearing of the Saviour is closely linked to 2:11, 13. Philanthropy still holds its original meaning in English: love for mankind. It always displays itself in action, not mere sentimentality. Paul had written more fully about this to the church at Ephesus (cf. Eph. 1:11-14; 2:4-7). In Hellenistic culture philanthropy was regarded as 'an essential attribute of a wise and effective ruler'.[246]

> This makes it probable that, here as elsewhere in these letters, the Apostle is deliberately modelling his language on

---

[245] Perkins, *The Pastoral Letters*, 276.
[246] Perkins, *The Pastoral Letters*, 276.

that of the contemporary ruler-cults in order to assert the more impressively the claims of Christianity.[247]

3:5 in Detail

οὐκ ἐξ ἔργων τῶν ἐν δικαιοσύνῃ ἃ ἐποιήσαμεν ἡμεῖς ἀλλὰ κατὰ τὸ αὐτοῦ ἔλεος ἔσωσεν ἡμᾶς
He saved us, not on the basis of deeds which we did in righteousness,

In verses 5-7 we see a critical description of 'grace alone' as Martin Luther would have it.

Not the labour of my hands
Can fulfill Thy law's demands;
Could my zeal no respite know,
Could my tears forever flow,
All could never sin erase,
Thou must save, and save by grace.

Nothing in my hands I bring,
Simply to Thy cross I cling
Naked, come to Thee for dress,
Helpless, look to Thee for grace:
Foul, I to the fountain fly,
Wash me, Saviour, or I die.
'Rock of Ages', A. M. Toplady

There is a deliberate contrast between 'he' and 'we' in this verse regarding the source of salvation. The Greek text is actually reversed in the English translation in NASB. The Greek says: 'Not because of righteous works that *we* did, *he* saved us.' To put matters beyond doubt, the Greek is quite emphatic in its use of ἐποιήσαμεν ἡμεῖς (*epoiēsamen hēmeis*): what *we did*. The placing of the subject

[247] Kelly, *Commentary on the Pastoral Epistles*, 251.

(ἡμεῖς) at the end of this clause gives it some prominence. What we did is completely contrary to what God wants and is the issue that God fixes by Christ's shed blood (cf. Is. 64:6).

> The meaning is 'we did', not 'we had done', which would imply works done prior to God's saving action. ... The translation 'have done' might erroneously seem to refer to works after the new birth. This verb as well as its subject 'we', is emphatic since it precedes the emphatic subject.[248]

The critical phrase is: '***HE*** *SAVED US!*' Grace was again at work through God's choice according to His sovereign will. There is nothing that any person can do to merit God's favour as far as salvation and eternal life are concerned (cf. John 3:36; Rom. 5:21). It is all of grace, as noted in the following phrase in this verse. This is the essence of Reformed theology.

διὰ λουτροῦ παλιγγενεσίας καὶ ἀνακαινώσεως πνεύματος ἁγίου,

but according to His mercy, by the washing of regeneration and renewing by the Holy Spirit,

Grace and mercy are closely tied together in God's character. Once again, Paul uses *but* because there is a distinct contrast between what we did and what God did. Grace and mercy flowed from a loving God who wants to redeem sinners. This was the good news (gospel) for the Cretans. Because of God's mercy he washed their sins away through regeneration and renewal by the Holy Spirit. A person's conversion to have faith in Christ has both positive and negative aspects. The person is 'washed' (λουτρόν – *loutron*): a cleansing from sin and the provision of forgiveness. Some commentators link this washing with the water of baptism but this is unneces-

[248] Greenlee, *Titus and Philemon*, 84.

sary, although it may be metaphorical. 'For a measured interpretive paraphrase, see Calvin, 382: "God saves us by his mercy, and He has given us a symbol and pledge of this salvation in baptism, by admitting us into His Church and engrafting us into the Body of His Son."'[249] The Holy Spirit, not baptism, is the agent of regeneration. Baptism is only an outward sign of an inward process. Water is simply an analogy for cleansing (of anything).

> 4 But God, being rich in mercy, because of His great love with which He loved us,
> 5 even when we were dead in our transgressions, made us alive together with Christ (by grace you have been saved),
> 6 and raised us up with Him, and seated us with Him in the heavenly *places* in Christ Jesus,
> 7 so that in the ages to come He might show the surpassing riches of His grace in kindness toward us in Christ Jesus.
> Ephesians 2:4-7 NASB

The really meaningful words in this phrase are regeneration (παλιγγενεσία - *palingenesia*) and renewal (ἀνακαίνωσις - *anakaiōsis*). I. H. Marshall comments that

> v 5b depicts the Holy Spirit as the source of the 'washing' which results in a transformation characterised here from the dual perspective of 'regeneration' and 'renewal'. The genitive is one of author or cause (Spicq, 654). The single preposition and conceptual closeness of 'regeneration' and 'renewal' suggest unity. The one event of salvation is viewed specifically from the standpoint of the work of the Holy Spirit. While the rite of water baptism may not be far from mind (as a symbolic expression depicting the work of the Spirit), it is that which it signifies — the individual's

[249] Yarbrough, *Letters to Timothy and Titus*, 546, n 285. The citation for Calvin is Calvin, *The Second Epistle of Paul the Apostle to the Corinthians and the Epistles to Timothy, Titus and Philemon*, 382.

> experience of the Spirit – that is the primary focal point, and this is probably linked with the paradigmatic experience of the Church at Pentecost (v 6, ἐξχέω). … *this is not a prooftext for baptismal regeneration or sacramental salvation.*[250]

Regeneration refers to new life in plants, animals and humans. In a Christian context, it refers to the new life (being born again spiritually) that comes from faith in Jesus as Saviour and Redeemer. Jesus spoke of this to Nicodemus: 'Truly, truly, I say to you, unless one is born of water *and the Spirit* he cannot enter into the kingdom of God.' (John 3:5, emphasis added); (cf. Eph. 5:26; 1 John 2:29). Renewal speaks of the new life that comes from the new birth. So, one follows the other. Both terms speak of the 'new creation' described in 1 Corinthians 5:17.

3:6 in Detail

οὗ ἐξέχεεν[251] ἐφ' ἡμᾶς πλουσίως διὰ ἰησοῦ χριστοῦ τοῦ σωτῆρος ἡμῶν,
whom He poured out upon us richly through Jesus Christ our Saviour,

The Holy Spirit was 'poured out' on Christians, and always is. The God of the Bible is a generous god (cf. 1 Chron. 29:14; Matt. 20:15). This pouring out of the Spirit is not a dribble from a partially opened tap but an abundant volume (cf. Acts 1:18; Rev. 16:1-4). The adjective πλουσίως (*plousiōs*) and its cognate words describe great riches (cf. Joel 2:28-29; Acts 2:17-18, 33; 1 Tim. 6:17).[252] The Spirit is given by Jesus Christ, as he taught his disciples in the gospel of John: 7:38-39; 15:26; 16:13. It is interesting that Paul

250 Marshall with Towner, *The Pastoral Epistles*, 321-22 (emphasis added).

251 Some Greek texts (e.g. UBS) do not use ἐξέχεεν but substitute the verb ἐκχέω which has the same meaning.

252 See Yarbrough, *Letters to Timothy and Titus*, 547-48.

notes the outpouring of the Holy Spirit by the Saviour (the ascended Christ). At the beginning of 3:4 God is described as Saviour and at the end of 3:6 Christ is described as Saviour. Paul has no doubt about the divinity of Jesus.

3:7 in Detail

ἵνα δικαιωθέντες τῇ ἐκείνου χάριτι κληρονόμοι γενηθῶμεν κατ᾽ ἐλπίδα ζωῆς αἰωνίου.
so that being justified by His grace we would be made heirs according to the hope of eternal life.

'Now comes the ultimate purpose, and, in effect, the results of God's act. It is theological, not ethical!'[253] There is a reason for this extraordinary gift from God to believers. An important contrast needs to be drawn between 'righteousness' in 3:5 and 'being justified' (δικαιόω – *dikaioō*) in this verse. Earlier, people were trying to make themselves acceptable to God for eternal life by performing 'righteous' deeds. This was utterly futile given God's holiness and their sinfulness. God provided the solution by giving his own Son to be crucified (John 3:16) and raising Him from the dead to prove Jesus' purity, holiness and power to defeat sin, death and hell. Justification involves the forgiveness of sins and being put in a right relationship with God; i.e. being clothed with Christ's righteousness and not our own. It is a once-for-all-time transaction.[254] By contrast with our former life, God justifies believers by his grace (and mercy) so that they gain the right to become his children (cf. John 1:12). Even more remarkably, God's justified children become 'heirs' (κληρονόμος – *klēronomos*) of the kingdom of God along with Christ himself! (cf.

[253] Marshall with Towner, *The Pastoral Epistles*, 323.
[254] See F. A. Schaeffer, *The Church Before the Watching World* in F. A. Schaeffer, *The Complete Works of Francis A. Schaeffer: A Christian Worldview*, 5 vols. (Wheaton, IL: Crossway, 1982), vol. 4, 176-77.

Rom. 8:17). The placement of this word before the verb gives it prominence. Paul notes that these heirs have the hope of eternal life. The word 'heirs' is closely related to the word 'inheritance', which has deep significance in the OT, being mentioned from Genesis to Malachi (cf. 1 Chron. 16:15-18; Ezra 9:12). However, the Bible says nothing about the content of our heavenly inheritance (cf. Rom. 4:14; 8:17; Gal. 3:29). Hope has been considered and explained at 2:13. It is something beyond doubt.

> One further clarification is necessary, and one that is almost universally missed: 'when the goodness and philanthropy of God ... appeared' (v 4) does not refer to the time when a person believes. The language is inappropriate for that event, and the corporate nature of the creed insists that it refer to the possibility of salvation accomplished by Christ's coming, his death, and resurrection. When the creed speaks of 'he saved us ... poured out for us ... having been justified ... we might become heirs', the time frame has not shifted. These statements are to be interpreted in light of the time frame established by v 4. Despite the use of personal pronouns, they are not speaking of the individual's appropriation of salvation, a fact supported using plural pronouns and the purpose clause rather than an indicative statement in v 7 (e.g. 'and we were justified and we became heirs'). The plural personal pronouns personalise God's intentions, spelling out why he did what he did, but the focus is still on God and his labours and intentions. The focus should not be shifted to the believer.[255]

Guthrie notes that 'The point of this reference to justification is that no one who is not justified can hope for an inheritance, and there is no doubt Paul would have consented to such a statement (cf. Galatians 3, which begins with justification, 3:11, and ends with inheritance, 3:29).'[256] Verses 5-7 are the essence of Reformed theology.

---

[255] Mounce, *Pastoral Epistles*, 438.

[256] Guthrie, *The Pastoral Epistles*, 206-07.

3:8 in Detail

πιστὸς ὁ λόγος,
This is a trustworthy statement,

The Greek text is to the point: 'Faithful the word.' It could be translated as 'These words you may trust' (NEB). Paul is referring to vv 4-7, which is a doctrinal statement in the letter (like its predecessors in 1 Timothy 1:15; 3:1; 4:9; 2 Timothy 2:11) concerning salvation. These words underline the significance of vv 4-7 as an important foundation for the hope of eternal life for believers, the sovereignty of God in choosing them, and the generosity of Christ through the Holy Spirit. These verses are decidedly Trinitarian in their exposition of the wonder of God's grace and mercy.

καὶ περὶ τούτων βούλομαί σε διαβεβαιοῦσθαι, ἵνα φροντίζωσιν καλῶν ἔργων προΐστασθαι οἱ πεπιστευκότες θεῷ.
and I want you to stress these things, so that those who have believed God will concentrate on being careful to engage in good deeds.

The NASB translation of διαβεβαιοῦσθαι (*diabebaiousthai*) as 'confidently' understates the strength of Paul's wish for Titus. The word (cf. 1 Tim. 1:7) has an emphasis of 'insisting emphatically' or 'stressing'. There is a need for Titus to press home to the Cretan Christians that the good behaviour described above in chapters 2 and 3 are imperative if their belief in God is genuine. The linking of this word with φροντίζω (*phrontizō*), meaning 'to give careful thought' or 'concentrate on', indicates that Titus really had to emphasise that Christian living and Christian belief (doctrine) go together.[257]

[257] See Zerwick and Grosvenor, *Analysis of the Greek New Testament*, vol. 2, 650. Titus is to give his mind to, and apply careful attention to, this trustworthy statement.

ταῦτά ἐστιν καλὰ καὶ ὠφέλιμα τοῖς ἀνθρώποις·
These things are good and profitable for men.

> When Christians exalt the Word of God and demonstrate God's power to transform lives, these things are good and profitable for men — for the believers themselves and, even more significantly as far as the emphasis of this passage is concerned, for the unsaved sinners around them who are drawn to Christ by the exemplary lives of those He has graciously transformed.[258]

The profitability (ὠφέλιμος - *ōphelimos*) of good deeds is that they are spiritually uplifting for the doer and beneficial to others, whether or not they are Christians.

3:9 in Detail

μωρὰς δὲ ζητήσεις καὶ γενεαλογίας καὶ ἔρεις καὶ μάχας νομικὰς περιΐστασο, εἰσὶν γὰρ ἀνωφελεῖς καὶ μάταιοι.
But avoid foolish controversies and genealogies and strife and disputes about the Law, for they are unprofitable and worthless.

Another '*but*' is inserted as a note of warning to Titus. Paul describes four things that Titus should avoid. Although he must insist that the Cretan Christians live useful, godly lives, Titus himself must avoid certain entanglements. These include unhelpful and foolish controversies and unnecessary arguments. Strife or discord is common to all human associations and the church is no different in this regard. It always has been, and always will be, difficult to maintain harmonious relations between people of differing opinions (cf. Ps. 120:7). Grace is the divine thread to mend these issues. The reference to genealogies is explained by Yarbrough.

[258] MacArthur, *1-2 Timothy and Titus*, 157.

> Ancestral descent is of undoubted significance in a religion that traces human origins to Adam and Eve, covenantal redemption to Abraham, and the giving of divine guidance (*tôrâ*) to the world through Moses. Jesus claimed to be descended from God, which his detractors denied, grounding their legitimacy in the heritage of Moses and claiming Jesus was actually of Samaritan descent (John 8:48-59). Paul claimed that believers were children of Abraham (Gal. 3), though some in the church (to say nothing of the Jews outside) insisted that adherence to circumcision and the law of Moses were necessary for salvation (Acts 15:1, 5). … Paul tells Timothy to instruct the Ephesian believers not 'to devote themselves to myths and endless genealogies', because 'such things promote controversial speculations rather than advancing God's work' (1 Tim. 1:4). Genealogies were not just an issue in Crete. Titus should take steps to avoid becoming enmeshed in debates about them.[259]

Clearly, this is a reference to those Jewish Christians who would not dispense with needless arguments about irrelevant issues concerning Jewish practices. Of course, with the number of Jews in the Cretan congregations, disputes about the Law of Moses would be a common reason for tension. The arguments were probably not so much about technicalities in the Mosaic Law itself so much as the relevance of the Law in a Christian context. We see this particularly in 1:10 where some of the chief troublemakers are obsessed with the need for circumcision. Paul advises that, after two warnings, Titus should not have anything to do with such people (3:10), who are unprofitable (ἀνωφελής - *anōphelēs*) for sensible conversation or discussion. It may be a word play by Paul to use *ōphelimos* (profitable) in v 8 and *anōphelēs* (unprofitable) in v 9. They are also 'worthless' (μάταιος - *mataios*), a word used in 1:10 (in the compound *mataiologoi* (cf. 1 Tim. 1:6)) for those

[259] Yarbrough, *Letters to Timothy and Titus*, 553.

opponents who are full of meaningless talk (cf. Acts 14:15; 1 Cor. 3:20; 15:17).

3:10 in Detail

αἱρετικὸν ἄνθρωπον μετὰ μίαν καὶ δευτέραν νουθεσίαν παραιτοῦ,
Reject a factious man after a first and second warning,

A factious man (αἱρετικός ἄνθρωπος - *hairetikos anthrōpos*) is one who divides a church. From this word we derive 'heretic' in English but here an appropriate description would be 'separatist'. This occurred in earliest Christianity when Gentile Jews complained about Aramaic-speaking Jews concerning the distribution of food (Acts 6:1). That matter was settled. In the Corinthian church Paul had to contend with factions based on personality (1 Cor. 3:4, 22). In the present case Jews were creating factions based on foolish Jewish myths (1:9). After two warnings, Titus is instructed to have nothing to do with factious people. We are given no hint of what comes next: whether it is simply ignoring them, or social exclusion, or even excommunication. Our only clues lie in Paul's directions in Romans 16:17; 1 Corinthians 5:11. Nevertheless, some disciplinary action needed to occur if misbehaviour continued. It probably took the form of exclusion from the congregation, but not necessarily forever. Gloer desires that 'church discipline should always be redemptive in nature':[260] a high ideal with varied degrees of success in reality.

3:11 in Detail

εἰδὼς ὅτι ἐξέστραπται ὁ τοιοῦτος καὶ ἁμαρτάνει, ὢν αὐτοκατάκριτος.

---

[260] W. Gloer, *1 & 2 Timothy-Titus*. Smyth & Helwys Bible Commentary (Macon, GA: Smyth & Helwys, 2010), 90.

knowing that such a man is perverted and is sinning, being self-condemned.

The refusal of men to desist from their wrong actions or words displays a wilful determination to reject the truth of the gospel and the salvation offered by God. There is a strong presumption here in the use of εἰδὼς (from οἶδα – *oida*) meaning 'knowing'. It is equivalent to 'you may be sure': there will be no doubt about the person's culpability. Paul regards such a person as 'perverted' (ἐξέστραπται -*exestraptai*). No doubt, Paul was influenced by the repeated condemnation of perverted language in the OT (cf. Prov. 8:13; 10:31-32; 17:20; Jer. 3:21). Clearly, such a person is sinning and, thus, self-condemned (αὐτοκατάκριτος – *autokatakritos*), a NT *hapax*. Their sin itself condemns them. There is no place for such men in the church. The word perhaps has the 'meaning that what may have been unconscious error now becomes deliberate.'[261]

13 The fear of the LORD is to hate evil;
Pride and arrogance and the evil way
And the perverted mouth, I hate.
Proverbs 8:13 NASB

31 The mouth of the righteous flows with wisdom,
But the perverted tongue will be cut out.
32 The lips of the righteous bring forth what is acceptable,
But the mouth of the wicked what is perverted.
Proverbs 10:31-32 NASB

20 He who has a crooked mind finds no good,
And he who is perverted in his language falls into evil.
Proverbs 17:20 NASB

261 Zerwick and Grosvenor, *Analysis of the Greek New Testament*, vol. 2, 651.

They might blame Titus or Paul or the church or even God, but their woes are the result of their own stubborn stance and refusal to back down in the face of what they will not recognise as truer understanding.[262]

Personal Concerns

3:12 *When I send Artemas or Tychicus to you, make every effort to come to me at Nicopolis, for I have decided to spend the winter there.*
3:13 *Diligently help Zenas the lawyer and Apollos on their way so that nothing is lacking for them.*
3:14 *Our people must also learn to engage in good deeds to meet pressing needs, so that they will not be unfruitful.*
3:15 *All who are with me greet you. Greet those who love us in the faith. Grace be with you all.*
NASB

3:12 in Detail

ὅταν πέμψω ἀρτεμᾶν πρὸς σὲ ἢ τυχικόν, σπούδασον ἐλθεῖν πρός με εἰς νικόπολιν, ἐκεῖ γὰρ κέκρικα παραχειμάσαι.
When I send Artemas or Tychicus to you, make every effort to come to me at Nicopolis, for I have decided to spend the winter there.

In concluding his letter, Paul now turns to a few personal matters which involve Titus. Paul asks Titus to join him in Nicopolis. The use of the aorist imperative of σπουδάζω (*spoudazō*) indicates that there is a sense of real urgency in Paul's request once the visitor has arrived in Crete. The sooner the visitor could establish himself in Titus' place, the sooner Titus could travel to Paul. 'Although several cities have this name, the most probable location is in Epirus, a region located on the western coast of Greece

[262] Yarbrough, *Letters to Timothy and Titus*, 556.

and the site of the Actian games.'[263] Paul planned to spend the winter there. Clearly, Paul was not in prison at this time. Paul plans to send Artemas or Tychicus[264] (Acts 20:3-4; Eph. 6:21-22; Col. 4:7-9; 2 Tim. 4:12) to replace Titus. 'Assuming the plan held good, apparently it was Artemas who replaced Titus – not Tychicus, who is placed in Ephesus in 2 Timothy 4:12. With the arrival of his replacement, Titus was able to make his way to Nicopolis, where Paul planned to spend the winter'.[265] The tense of the Greek verb κρίνω (*kekrika* - 'decided') indicates that Paul had already decided on this course of action.[266]

> Paul's decision to spend the winter in Nicopolis favours that the commanded diligence includes Titus' coming before winter's onset. For sailing during winter, as Titus would have to do when leaving the island of Crete, was dangerous and usually avoided (see Acts 27 for Paul's recognition of the danger, involving Crete). So the commanded diligence in a sending of Zenas the lawyer and Apollos is also likely to include action taken before winter's onset (compare 2 Tim. 4:9, 21).[267]

Artemas' name is related to the Greek god, Artemis (Acts 19:24), being a shortened form of Ἀρτεμίδορος - (*Artemidoros*), meaning 'gift of Artemis'.[268] We know

---

[263] Perkins, *Pastoral Letters*, 284. Barclay, *The Letters to Timothy, Titus and Philemon*, 265 notes that Nicopolis was in Epirus and was 'the best centre for work in the Roman province of Dalmatia'.

[264] His name means 'fortunate'.

[265] Towner, *1-2 Timothy and Titus*, 263.

[266] Perkins, *Pastoral Letters*, 285. Page 221 refers to the use of this verb in 2 Tim. 4:1 and comments that 'These are the only occurrences of this verb in the PE [Pastoral Epistles]'.

[267] Gundry. *Commentary on First and Second Timothy, Titus*, 72.

[268] Marshall with Towner, *Pastoral Epistles*, 341; Perkins, *Pastoral Letters*, 284. Yarbrough, *Letters to Timothy and Titus*, 556 comments that Artemas 'was a common name, not to be confused with the female goddess Artemis'.

nothing more about Artemas;[269] but the fact that he could minister to the Cretan Christians in the absence of Titus speaks volumes for his faith, capacity and Paul's confidence in him.

3:13 in Detail

ζηνᾶν τὸν νομικὸν καὶ ἀπολλῶν σπουδαίως πρόπεμψον, ἵνα μηδὲν αὐτοῖς λείπῃ.
Diligently help Zenas the lawyer and Apollos on their way so that nothing is lacking for them.

Titus was asked to equip for further journeys Zenas the lawyer and Apollos, the eloquent and learned teacher from Alexandria to whom Prisca and Aquila had given instruction at Ephesus (Acts 18:24-25). A party of Corinthians also claimed him as their leader (Acts 19:1; 1 Cor. 1:12; 3:4-6, 22; 4:6; 16:12). These were important officials for whom Titus was responsible for greeting and resourcing. They were to be warmly received and outfitted for their continued journey. It seems unlikely that Titus would not be diligent (i.e. willing) in assisting Zenas and Apollos on their way. It seems appropriate to translate σπουδαίως (*spoudaiōs*) as meaning both 'with diligence and alacrity' (cf. 3:12). The logical conclusion is that Zenas and Apollos were visiting Titus on Crete before travelling elsewhere. Unless they were with Titus personally, he could not have been able to fulfil their needs as thoroughly as Paul requested.

> He [Apollos] seems to have ministered cooperatively but independently from Paul. Since Paul addresses Titus alone, at the time of writing Zenas and Apollos have yet to arrive in Crete. They're probably carrying Paul's letter

[269] See W. Barclay, *The Letters to Timothy, Titus and Philemon*. The Daily Study Bible. revised edition. Edinburgh: St Andrew Press 1975, 265; Gundry, *Commentary on First and Second Timothy, Titus*, 72.

> to Titus. But Paul wants them to rejoin him. Titus' sending forward Zenas and Apollos while he himself waits for the arrival of Artemas or Tychicus before going himself to Paul — this sending forward includes supplying Zenas and Apollos with whatever they need for their journey to Paul: food, money, and such like. And for a supply that will leave nothing lacking, Cretan Christians (whom Paul calls 'our [people]') are 'to be engaging in good deeds', which in this case means supplying Zenas's and Apollos's 'essential needs'. These Cretans will be learning by the actual doing (cf. 1 Tim. 5:4, 13). ' Also to be learning' seems to mean learning by doing as well as learning by listening to Titus' exhortations.[270]

Zenas is a shortened form of Zenodorus, a Greek name meaning 'gift of Zeus'.[271] Having a Greek name with reference to a pagan god implies that Zenas was a god-fearer — a Gentile converted to Judaism. He is described as 'the lawyer' (ὁ νομικός - *ho nomikos*), which can refer to an expert in the Jewish law or an expert in Greek or Roman law. The word is otherwise used in the NT only in the gospels of Matthew and Luke, where the references are to experts in the Law of Moses. However, Paul uses it twice in his letter to Titus. In Titus 3:9 νομικὸς is used regarding disputes about the Law of Moses. If Zenas was a Gentile, and given his linkage to Apollos in this verse, it may be the case that Zenas was skilled in Jewish law. However, Scott[272] came to the opposite conclusion, as did Marshall. 'The relation of his name to that of the Greek god Zeus ("Zenas" meaning "a gift of Zeus") favours that he didn't come from Jewish stock and therefore had legal

[270] Gundry. *Commentary on First and Second Timothy, Titus*, 72-73. Despite Gundry's assertion, there is no indication that Paul wants Zenas and Apollos to join him. It is Titus who Paul wishes to see.

[271] HSIBD, 1121.

[272] E. F. Scott. *The Pastoral Epistles*. MNTC. (London: Hodder and Stoughton 1936), 181.

expertise outside Jewish law.'[273] 'The word in itself does not indicate what kind of law is meant, whether Jewish, Greek or Roman law but a Jewish lawyer is unlikely with such a pagan name (*pace* Lock)'.[274]

> What of 'Zenas the lawyer' (3:13)? Otherwise unknown in the NT, he has been variously identified as an expert in Jewish law, or, as his pagan name might suggest, a Roman lawyer. In fact it was common for lawyers to visit Crete in Roman times. The famous stone panels on which were inscribed the Law Code of Gortyn dated from c 450 BCE but had been restored under Roman rule and were prominently displayed to facilitate study. Crete became 'a centre of pilgrimage for legal inspiration'.[275]

'Since he [Apollos] was from Alexandria, it is suggested that he and Zenas may have been heading in a southerly direction from Paul, to Crete, and then finally on to Alexandria. This is only a possibility, however'.[276] Regarding Apollos' presence on Crete, Wieland comments:

> It was not only Alexandrians who might be predisposed to 'stupid controversies, genealogies, dissensions, and quarrels about the law' (Titus 3.9), but if the sort of Hellenistic Judaism that flourished in Alexandria furnished part of the environment envisaged by the author, who better to help than Apollos (Titus 3:13), the learned Alexandrian Jew encountered in Acts 18.24-28; 1 Cor. 3.4-6, and so on?[277]

We do not know the fate of Apollos.

---

[273] Gundry, *Commentary on First and Second Timothy, Titus*, 72.

[274] Marshall with Towner, *Pastoral Epistles,* p. 343. See Yarbrough, *Letters to Timothy and Titus*, 557; Gundry, *Commentary on First and Second Timothy, Titus*, 62 for agreement.

[275] Wieland, *Roman Crete and the Letter to Titus*, p. 353.

[276] Yarbrough, *Letters to Timothy and Titus*, 557.

[277] G. M. Wieland. 'Roman Crete and the Letter to Titus' *NTS* vol. 53, no. 3 (2009): 353.

3:14 in Detail

μανθανέτωσαν δὲ καὶ οἱ ἡμέτεροι καλῶν ἔργων προΐστασθαι εἰς τὰς ἀναγκαίας χρείας, ἵνα μὴ ὦσιν ἄκαρποι.
Our people must also learn to engage in good deeds to meet pressing needs, so that they will not be unfruitful.

The Cretans were to learn (μανθάνω - *manthanō*) to display good deeds (cf. 1 Tim. 2:11; 5:4). The inclusion of τὰς indicates that Titus knows the nature of these 'pressing needs'. This is supposed to be an ongoing process. By such acts the Cretan Christians were to make themselves useful in relation to these pressing needs. Paul uses the words ἀναγκαίας and χρεὶας (*anagkaias* and *chreias*) to refer to daily necessities, things people really needed (cf. Rom. 12:13; Phlp. 4:16). In a comment about Acts 3:45-46, Schaeffer observes:

> Note, too, that deacons were appointed. Why? Because the church had found difficulty in caring for one another's material needs. Read James 2. James asks, 'What are you doing preaching the gospel to a man and trying to have a good relationship with him spiritually if he needs shoes and you do not give him shoes?' Here is another place where the awful Platonic element in the evangelical church has been so dominant and so deadly. It has been considered spiritual to give to missions, but not equally spiritual to give when my brother needs shoes. That is never found in the Word of God. Of course, the early church gave to missions; at times they gave money so Paul did not have to make tents. But Paul makes no distinction between collections for missions and collections for material needs, as if one were spiritual and the other not. For the most part when Paul spoke of financial matters, he did so because there was a group of Christians somewhere who had a material need, and Paul then called upon other churches to help.[278]

[278] F. A. Schaeffer, *Two Contents, Two Realities* in F. A. Schaeffer, *The Complete Works of Francis A. Schaeffer: A Christian Worldview*, 5 vols.

By being responsive in such situations, the Christian community is being given opportunity to grow in grace and thereby to welcome the reconciling power of the Spirit in their lives.[279] The worldwide fellowship of Christians is expressed in Paul's description of the Cretan Christians (who accord with Titus' directions) as '*our* people' (οἱ ἡμέτεροι – *hoi hēmeteroi*).

As Paul ends his letter, he returns to its main theme: Christianity must involve faith and practice. It is not a theoretical religion but demonstrably practical and useful to the church and society for salvation and the benefit of others. Given the nature of Cretan society in general, the young age of the church and the presence of opponents, Titus is again urged to set right what remains to be done (1:5). 'Christians must learn that good works, specifically those that provide for people with pressing needs, must be the logical and natural extension of submitting to the salvation and Lordship of Christ.'[280]

3:15 in Detail

ἀσπάζονταί σε οἱ μετ᾽ ἐμοῦ πάντες. ἄσπασαι τοὺς φιλοῦντας ἡμᾶς ἐν πίστει.
All who are with me greet you. Greet those who love us in the faith.

This letter is sent with greetings from all those brothers and sisters who were with Paul. This is the application of Paul's message to Titus that the church (God's people together) does good works as well as individuals. Most, if not all, of these people would have met Titus and they are

(Wheaton, IL: Crossway, 1982), vol. 3, 421.

279 See T. C. Oden, *First and Second Timothy and Titus: Interpretation: A Bible Commentary for Teaching and Preaching*. reprinted 2012 (Louisville: Westminster John Knox, 1989), 165.

280 Mounce, *Pastoral Epistles*, 460.

as enthusiastic as Paul about the work that Titus is pursuing. φιλοῦντας (*philountas*) means 'love as friends'.

> The conclusion of Titus is addressed to ὑμῶν, 'you,' plural: 'Grace be with all of you' (3:15). This shows that despite its form as a personal epistle, it is written for public dissemination. Like 1 Timothy, it is an official validation of Titus' mission and a clarification of specific tasks. The lack of personal comments can also be accounted for by the historical situation. Titus may have been older, more mature, and therefore less prone to depression and the need for encouragement than was Timothy. The Cretan situation was also less serious [than was the case with Timothy in Ephesus] and Titus was in less danger.[281]

The people on Crete to whom greetings are sent are those who are real Christians: the 'our people' of v 14.

ἡ χάρις μετὰ πάντων ὑμῶν.
Grace be with you all.

The beginning and end of this letter resound with 'grace' to Titus (cf. 1:5) and his fellow Christians. 'Amazing grace, how sweet the sound!' (John Newton)

281 Mounce, *Pastoral Epistles*, 385.

IMPLICATIONS FOR TODAY'S CHURCHES

The instructions by the apostle Paul to Titus were written in the context of Crete in the first century AD. The social, if not the economic, framework of Crete at that time bears a disturbingly similar comparison to our situation in the Western world today. The issues *Titus* addresses have compelling relevance to the state of many Protestant churches in the West.[282] Generally, African and Asian churches are more orthodox and conservative, and taking a more robust response to liberalism. However, it seems that liberalism is making inroads in more modernised places such as Singapore.

As was written earlier, *Titus* warns about a cancer that is ravaging the body of Christ in the twenty-first century. As with cancer in a human body, the cancer of liberal morality, theology and doctrine, based on a repudiation of the truth and validity of the Bible, must be identified and then excised emphatically with the sword of the Word of God. This is the only way that the body can be restored to health. Otherwise, the body of Christ will survive (John 10:28) only as a broken reed (Isa. 42:3), rather than a tree firmly planted by streams of living water (Ps. 1:3). The church in the West is at a stage where radical surgery is

[282] There is no room here to comment on the Roman Catholic or Orthodox churches because their theology, culture and practices are far removed from what Paul was writing about in *Titus*.

essential. Even amputations of some leadership may be necessary if the body is to survive.

This has critical implications for Christians individually and the church generally in the twenty-first century. There is no doubt that since the late 18th century liberal theology, originating with the 'higher criticism' of German theologians, has widely infiltrated the church (especially through false teaching in many theological seminaries and, eventually, from pulpits) and has cast a deep shadow over 'the faith' that Paul and Titus espoused. At the present time, 'the faith' of the Bible is accepted by a smaller proportion of Christians in the Western world, who not only call themselves *but are* 'Bible-believing Christians'. Acceptance of the inerrancy of Scripture is one of the greatest hurdles that the church must overcome if the validity of its message is to have any resonance in a deeply sinful Western culture. Francis Schaeffer recognised this forty years ago but since then things have only deteriorated. Can it be reversed?

> **Does inerrancy make a difference? Overwhelmingly; the difference is that with the Bible being what it is, God's Word and so absolute, God's objective truth, we do not need to be, *and we should not be,* caught in the ever-changing fallen cultures which surround us. Those who do not hold the inerrancy of Scripture do not have this high privilege.** To some extent, they are at the mercy of the fallen changing culture. And Scripture is thus bent to conform to the changing world spirit of the day, and they therefore have no solid authority upon which to judge and to resist the views and values of that changing, shifting world spirit.[283]

The other major difficulty is the proper interpretation of Scripture (hermeneutics). Westminster Theological

---

[283] F. A. Schaeffer, *The Great Evangelical Disaster*. (Westchester, IL: Crossway, 1984), 61 (emphasis added).

Seminary in Philadelphia was founded by scholars who rejected increasing liberalism in Christian theology and belief. I quote from part of the opening address of J. Gresham Machen, its first president, on 25 September 1929:

> If, then, the students of our seminary can read the Bible not merely in translations, but as it was given by the Holy Spirit to the church, then they are prepared to deal intelligently with the question what the Bible means. There we have the great subject of biblical exegesis or biblical interpretation. I hesitate to use that word 'interpretation', for it is a word that has been the custodian of more nonsense, perhaps, than any other word in the English language today. Every generation, it is said, must interpret the Bible and the creeds of the church in its own way. So it is said in effect by many modern leaders of the church: 'We accept the Apostles' Creed, but we must interpret the Apostles' Creed in a way that will suit the modern mind. So we repeat the assertion of the Creed, "The third day He rose again from the dead," but we interpret that to mean, "The third day He did not rise again from the dead."'
>
> *In the presence of this modern business of interpreting perfectly plain assertions to mean their exact opposite, do you know what I verily believe? I verily believe that the new Reformation, for which we long, will be like the Reformation of the sixteenth century in that it will mean a return to plain common honesty and common sense.* At the end of the middle ages the Bible had become a book with seven seals; it had been covered with the rubbish of the fourfold sense of Scripture and all that. The Reformation brushed that rubbish away. So again today the Bible has been covered with an elaborate business of 'interpretation' that is worse in some respects than anything that the middle ages could produce. The new Reformation will brush all that away. There will be a rediscovery of the great Reformation doctrine of the perspicuity of Scripture; *men will make the astonishing discovery that the Bible is a plain book addressed to plain men, and that it means exactly what it says.*

> In our work in exegesis at Westminster Seminary, at any rate, we shall seek to cultivate common sense. But common sense is not so common as is sometimes supposed, and for the cultivation of it true learning is not out of place. What a world of vagaries, what a sad waste of time, could be avoided if men would come into contact with the truly fine exegetical tradition of the Christian church! Such contact with the devout and learned minds of the past would not discourage freshness or originality. Far from it; it would help to shake us out of a rut and lead us into fields of fruitful thinking.
>
> ***In true biblical exegesis, the Bible must be taken as God has been pleased to give it to the church.***[284]

Leadership in the Church

Titus is particularly concerned about the appointment of elders to lead the Cretan churches.

Chapter 1 contains important guidance for twenty-first century Christians (individually and, particularly, churches) reading Paul's instructions regarding the appointment of elders (and pastors). His message can be split in two.

1. *Leadership Qualifications*

Paul describes clearly the qualifications for those who would be *appointed* as elders in the Cretan churches, which had recently been established during his and Titus' recent evangelical tour of the island. In the twenty-first century, the principles enunciated by Paul in *Titus* and 1 Timothy 3 must be applied to any church's leadership structure before individuals can be considered. These principles apply equally to the appointment of pastors of churches.

[284] J. G. Machen, 'Westminster Theological Seminary: Its Purpose and Plan' in *J Gresham Machen: Selected Shorter Writings*. Ed. D. G. Hart (Phillipsburg, NJ: P & R Publishing, 2004).

They are consistent with the instructions in his earlier letters to other newly formed Christian churches established in the Roman provinces of Greece and Asia. These are:

- Churches must be governed by several elders. This reflects Jesus' commitment that 'For where two or three are gathered in my name, there I am among them' (Matthew 18:20). The requirement in 1:5 is that Titus 'should appoint *elders* in *every* town' (καταστήσῃς κατὰ πόλιν πρεσβυτέρους - *katastēsēs kata polin presbuterous*). No church can be reliably governed by one elder alone, lest he fall into sin, gain a hunger for power or fall into error concerning the Word of God. The text clearly states that each church is to have several elders.
- These elders should be local, based in the town where the church is located. This enables them to know the members of the congregation and the society around them.
- Elders should be men. This reflects the divine instructions in Genesis 2 for male headship.[285] Verse 1:6 above uses ἀνήρ (*anēr*), which is the Greek word for a male person.

God's standards for leadership in the church are high, a basic and extremely crucial truth that many evangelical churches today either deny or ignore. New Testament standards are often lowered, or selectively applied, or simply disregarded. ***Some congregations and denominations pick and choose pastoral qualifications that seem most relevant and appropriate for the times, that satisfy personal preferences, and that do not conflict too sharply with contemporary social standards and practises.*** Some take the liberty to waive biblical standards when they like

[285] For a full explanation of this principle, see Manuell, *Gender Wars in Christianity*.

> a pastor, and the application of those standards might result in his dismissal. ***Nothing is more needed in the church than the careful application of biblical principles of leadership.*** Yet sound, qualified biblical leaders are alarmingly scarce in contemporary churches.[286]

The shepherd/pastor model for selecting ministers is more appropriate than the 'CEO' type, where consideration of age, style, presentability (to both congregation and the public), entertaining speaking ability, etc. crowds out faithfulness to gospel preaching and teaching.

2. ***Personal Characteristics***

Much emphasis is placed on the qualifications of elders in terms of 'dos and don'ts' (1:5-16). The list in 1:6-9 can be summarised by the word 'godliness'. All these personal characteristics conform to OT standards (in Titus' time) and to the qualities described by Paul and Peter in the NT (cf. 1 Tim. 3:2-7; 1 Pet. 5:4) regarding elders.

Modern denominations have 'elders' (including clergy) who are not free from accusation regarding their public (and, particularly, private) lifestyles. An example was the justified publicity given in recent years to serious misconduct by clergy and laity concerning child sexual abuse. In Australia, a Royal Commission exposed this flagrant abuse of power that was covered up by denominational administrators for decades.[287] Many offenders have escaped any punishment by the law or the church. When

[286] MacArthur, *1-2 Timothy and Titus,* 18 (emphasis added). See fuller comments in 18-20. The success (in Christian terms) of John MacArthur's church vindicates what he writes.

[287] The offenders came from all denominations but, particularly, the Roman Catholic church. That has also been the case in the United States. A recent revelation of serious sexual abuse of boys in the Anglican church in Africa by a white English minister decades ago caused the resignation of Justin Welby, Archbishop of Canterbury, who was aware of it and did nothing.

it comes to the gospel, the required level of morality for clergy and 'elders' must be rigorously enforced. We now have a situation in the western world where an openly homosexual relationship between two clerics (displayed at Synod) in the Anglican church in Melbourne, Australia goes without comment, let alone rebuke, by church leaders. Now that women have been ordained, we have the same behaviour with lesbian relationships. Although serious, there is no point dwelling just on sexual sin, as bad as that is. Others live lavish lifestyles in mansions, while others seek public approval by their close association with high-profile political, business or media people. The gospel seems to be secondary to their behaviour, company and lifestyles. For many Christian leaders (clergy and elders) their characters are far from blameless in the context of *Titus*.

There are egregious examples in Australia and, particularly, the United States, of pastors where the desire for monetary gain, fame, ambition as an entertainer, or to be the leader of a 'mega-church' has led to the pastor's downfall and disgrace.

> The pastor is not merely a social worker or religious organiser, nor is such ministry viewed from the standpoint of human self-actualisation or the self-directed deployment of spiritual gifts. The character, presence, and active will of God in the pastoral mission lay the highest necessity of probity on Titus and prospective appointees. Paul's point could have to do with the notion of God as judge in all this. He could also have in mind the high stakes and spiritual nature of the conflict churches face on Crete – the sanctity, if not survival, of God's work in the form of the church there is at stake, and divine resources are required for those who answer the bell to uphold God's truth and interests.[288]

[288] Yarbrough, *Letters to Timothy and Titus*, 483.

Titus needed divine assistance to perceive the underlying character of the potential candidates. Today, churches still need the wisdom of the Holy Spirit to assist in choosing elders and pastors. They need men of the highest probity.

Different Groups in the Church

In *Titus* Paul refers to the roles and needs of various groups within a church. He described natural divisions such as old and young, men and women, rich and poor. Nevertheless, these physical differences needed to be overlooked if the church was to function as one body in Christ (cf. Eph. 2:11-22; 4:3-6). Each member of a church has the capacity to contribute.

From a spiritual perspective, the variety of groups in a church might be categorised by gifts given by the Holy Spirit (cf. 1 Cor. 12:12-27). There will be teachers, those with the gift of administration (so necessary for elders), others whose ability to care and show compassion. Some will provide monetary assistance to keep the church functioning and to help the poor; others will be warriors in prayer. Paul informed the Corithian church:

> 4 There are varieties of gifts, but the same Spirit.
> 5 There are varieties of service, but the same Lord.
> 6 There are many forms of work, but all of them, in all men, are the work of the same God.
> 7 In each of us the Spirit is manifested in one particular way, for some useful purpose.
> 1 Corinthians 12:4-7 (NEB)

Each church should be united as one body in Christ, notwithstanding the various groups and spiritual gifts of the congregation. Mutual recognition and acceptance of these facts will enable each person to provide spiritual nourishment and strength to the body as a whole.

> 'In our age, where biblical teachings and practices have frequently been abandoned and where pastoral care seems often to be construed as only affirming the errant and seldom confronting them, Paul's words pose formidable challenge and in fact are clearly rejected by many.'[289]

Titus 1:14 is an especially important command for those twenty-first century churches where more than expository Bible preaching is delivered from some pulpits. Although it is inappropriate for pastors to tell their congregations to vote for particular political parties, for example, it is quite within their remit to teach in such a way as to make people aware of the biblical truths that ought to influence their political decisions.

Just as Titus was to denounce 'foolish controversies' (3:9) in Crete, we should expose falsehood in our own churches (hopefully led by wise elders), not being afraid of any shame or criticism that may be levelled at us. To be competent in making such judgments (when necessary), believers themselves need to be concerned for their own consistency with Scripture (in mind and body) to avoid damnation as hypocrites.

The principles Paul gave to Titus two thousand years ago still remain pertinent today regarding women. Older Christian women need to lead godly and wise lives, not getting caught up in day-to-day gossiping, but teaching and encouraging younger women (including their own daughters) to live kind, quiet lives and, if married, to be submissive to their husbands. Such women are the mainstay of many churches today and bring glory to God and honour to themselves by their demeanour in church and civil society. Mutual encouragement has always caused a group of women to be stronger than they are as individuals.

---

[289] Yarbrough, *Letters to Timothy and Titus*, 498.

Evangelism is Multifaceted

The most common understanding of 'evangelism' is the oral proclamation of the gospel of Christ to others, whether individually or in large groups. The most famous example of this type of evangelism in the twentieth century was the Billy Graham Crusade, which proclaimed the gospel to, and converted, millions of people around the world. At the other end of the spectrum, one by one, Christians also tell individuals about Jesus. Oral proclamation, in churches or to the next-door neighbour, is the most effective means of spreading the gospel message to people who need sins forgiven and the glorious hope of eternal life.

Although Paul encourages Titus to engage in this type of evangelism/teaching by speaking to the Cretans (2:1, 8; 3:8), much of the letter's emphasis is on practical evangelism by the Cretan Christians through their lifestyle (chapter 2; 3:8, 14). While there is a strong reference to the behaviour of elders, this does not exclude the remainder of the Christians in Crete from behaving in a God-honouring way. This is practical evangelism to our needy world.

Concluding Comments

Titus is still speaking to Christians in the twenty-first century. It provides much guidance on the criteria that churches should use in choosing pastors and elders under the direction of the Holy Spirit. There is wisdom for the behaviour of members of congregations: male and female; old and young; rich and poor. In a world obsessed by materialism, 'me' and various woke agendas (all of which deny the presence (let alone the power) of the God of the Bible), *Titus* is a reminder of God's intention over eternity.

So will My word which goes forth from My mouth;

It will not return to Me empty,
Without accomplishing what I desire,
And without succeeding in the matter for which I sent it.
Isaiah 55:11 NASB

God's word in *Titus* is still being sent out by Him nearly two thousand years after it was written. May it bless your understanding of the requirements for churches today, prescribed by the God who 'is the same yesterday, today and forever' (Heb. 13:8).

BIBLIOGRAPHY

Andersen, F. I., 'Yahweh, the Kind and Sensitive God,' in *God Who Is Rich in Mercy: Essays Presented to Dr D. B. Knox*. P. T. O'Brien and D. G. Peterson, editors (Homebush West, NSW: Lancer Books, 1986).

Barclay, W., *The Letters to Timothy, Titus and Philemon*. The Daily Study Bible. revised edition. (Edinburgh: St Andrew Press, 1975).

Barnett, C., *The Second Epistle to the Corinthians*. NICNT (Grand Rapids: Eerdmans, 1997).

Berkhof, L., *Systematic Theology* (Edinburgh: Banner of Truth, 1976).

Bray, G. L., *The Pastoral Epistles*. ITC (London: T. & T. Clark, 2019).

Brown, M. J., 'Paul's Use of ΔΟΥΛΟΣ ΧΡΙΣΤΟΥ ΙΗΣΟΥ in Romans 1:1,' *Journal of Biblical Literature* 120:4 (2001): 723-37.

Calvin, J., *The Second Epistle of Paul the Apostle to the Corinthians and the Epistles to Timothy, Titus and Philemon*. Translated by T. A. Smail. D. W. and T. F. Torrance, editors (Grand Rapids: Eerdmans, 1964).

Capill, M., *The Elder-Led Church: How an Eldership Team Shepherds a Healthy Flock* (Phillipsburg, NJ: Presbyterian & Reformed, 2024).

Chester, T., *Titus for You* (UK: The Good Book Company, 2014).

Coleman-Norton, R., *Studies in Roman Economic and Social History* (Princeton, NJ: Princeton University Press, 1951).

Crabb, Rachael and Raeann Hart, *The Personal Touch: Encouraging Others through Hospitality* (Colorado Springs, CO: NavPress, 1990).

Cranfield, C. E. B., *1 and 2 Peter and Jude*. Torch Bible Commentaries (London: SCM Press, 1960).

Davids, P. H., *The Letters of 2 Peter, Jude*. PNTC. Grand Rapids: Eerdmans, 2006).

Doriani, D. M. and R. D. Phillips, *2 Timothy and Titus* (Phillipsburg, NJ: P & R Publishing, 2020).

Dumbrell, W. J., *Covenant and Creation: An Old Testament Covenantal Theology* (Homebush West, NSW: Lancer Books, 1984).

Duncan, G. S. *The Epistle of Paul to the Galatians*. MNTC (London: Hodder and Stoughton, 1934).

Dunn, J. D. G., *Romans 9-16* (Dallas: Word Books, 1988).

– – –, 'Echoes of Intra-Jewish Polemic in Paul's Letter to the Galatians', *Journal of Biblical Literature*, 112:3 (1993): 459-77.

Fee, G. D., *1 & 2 Timothy, Titus*. Understanding the Bible Commentary Series. Revised edition (Grand Rapids: Baker Publishing Group, 2011).

Ferguson, S. B. and D. Wright (eds), *New Dictionary of Theology* (Leicester: Inter-Varsity Press, 1988).

Friberg, T., B. Friberg and N. F. Miller, *Analytical Lexicon of the Greek New Testament* (Grand Rapids: Baker Books, 2000).

Garlington, D. B., *An Exposition of Galatians: A New Perspective/Reformational Reading* (Eugene, OR: Wipf & Stock, 2003).

Gill, D. W. J., *A Saviour for the Cities of Crete: The Roman Background to the Epistle to Titus* in P. J. Williams, A. D. Clarke *et al.* (eds), *The New Testament in its First Century Setting: Essays on Context and Background in Honour of B. W. Winter on His 65th Birthday* (Grand Rapids: Eerdmans, 2004).

Gloer, W., *1 & 2 Timothy-Titus*. Smyth & Helwys Bible Commentary (Macon, GA: Smyth & Helwys, 2010).

Green, G. L., *Jude and 2 Peter*. Baker Exegetical Commentary on the New Testament (Grand Rapids: Baker Academic, 2008).

Greenlee, J. H., *An Exegetical Summary of Titus and Philemon*, second edition (Dallas: SIL International, 2008).

Gundry, R. H. *Commentary on First and Second Timothy, Titus* (Grand Rapids: Baker Academic, 2010).

Guthrie, D., *The Pastoral Epistles*. TNTC (Leicester: Inter-Varsity Press, 1957).

– – – *The Second Epistle to the Corinthians: A Commentary on the Greek Text* (Grand Rapids: Eerdmans, 2005).

Harris, M. J., *Slave of Christ: A New Testament Metaphor for Total Devotion to Christ*. New Studies in Biblical Theology 8. (Downers Grove, IL: Inter-Varsity Press, 1999).

Hays, R. B., *The Faith of Jesus Christ: An Investigation of the Narrative Substructure of Galatians 3:1-4:11*. Society of Biblical Literature Dissertation Series 56 (Chico, CA.: Scholars Press, 1983).

Hiebert, D. E., *Titus and Philemon* (Chicago: Moody Publishers, 1957).

Hendriksen, W., *Commentary on I and II Timothy and Titus* (London: Banner of Truth, 1959).

Henry, M., *The Complete works of Matthew Henry: Treatises, Sermons, and Tracts*. 2 vols. (Grand Rapids: Baker Books, reprinted 1979).

Houlden, J. L., *The Pastoral Epistles*. Penguin New Testament Commentary (London, SCM Press, 1989).

Lockyer, H. Snr. (general editor), *The Hodder and Stoughton Illustrated Bible Dictionary* (Nashville, TN: Hodder and Stoughton).

Jensen, P. F., *The Life of Faith: An Introduction to Christian Doctrine* (Sydney: Matthias Media, 2022).

Kelly, J. N. D., *A Commentary on the Pastoral Epistles*. Harper's New Testament Commentaries (London: Adam & Charles Black, 1963).

Kidd, R. M. ,'Titus as Apologia: Grace for Liars, Beasts, and Bellies'. *Horizons in Biblical Theology* 21 [1999] 185-209.

Köstenberger, A. J., *Commentary on 1-2 Timothy and Titus*. Biblical Theology for Christian Proclamation (Nashville, TN: Holman, 2017).

Kruse, C. G., *2 Corinthians: An Introduction and Commentary*. TNCT (Downers Grove, IL: Inter-Varsity Press, 2015).

Liefeld, W. L., *The NIV Application Commentary: 1 & 2 Timothy, Titus* (Grand Rapids: Zondervan, 1999).

Lenski, R. C. H., *The Interpretation of the Epistles of St Peter, St John and St Jude* (Minneapolis, MN: Augsburg Publishing House, 1966).

Long, T. G., *1 & 2 Timothy and Titus* (Louisville: Westminster John Knox, 2016).

Luther, M., *Luther's Works*, J. Pelikan (editor) (St Louis: Concordia, 1966).

MacArthur, J., *1-2 Timothy and Titus*. MacArthur New Testament Commentary (Chicago: Moody Publishers, 1996).

– – –, *1 and 2 Thessalonians*. MacArthur New Testament Commentary (Chicago: Moody Publishers, 2002).

Manuell, G., *Gender Wars in Christianity* (Brisbane: Connor Court, 2018).

– – –, *The Letter of Jude: A Wake-Up Call to Twenty-First Century Christians*, revised edition (Sydney: Tulip Publishing, 2022).

– – –, *The People in Paul's Letters: A Compendium of Characters* (Fearn: Christian Focus Publications, 2025).

Marshall, I. H., *The Epistles of John* (Grand Rapids: Eerdmans, 1978).

– – – with P. H. Towner, *A Critical and Exegetical Commentary on The Pastoral Epistles*. ICC (Edinburgh: T. & T. Clark, 1999).

Martin, R. P., *2 Corinthians*. WBC (Grand Rapids: Zondervan, 2014).

Moo, D. J., *Galatians*. BECNT (Grand Rapids: Baker Academic, 2013).

Morris, L. L., *The Apostolic Preaching of the Cross* (Leicester: Inter-Varsity Press, 1965).

Mounce, W. D., *Pastoral Epistles*. WBC (Grand Rapids: Thomas Nelson, 2000).

Muehlenberg, W., *Evangelical Pharisees and the God We Serve*. See 'CultureWatch' at *www.billmuehlenberg.com*, 7 May 2024.

Oden, T. C., *First and Second Timothy and Titus: Interpretation: A Bible Commentary for Teaching and Preaching*. reprinted 2012 (Louisville: Westminster John Knox Press, 1989).

Perkins, L. J., *The Pastoral Letters: a handbook on the Greek text*. Baylor Handbook on the Greek New Testament (Waco, TX: Baylor University Press, 2017).

Polybius, *Histories (6.46.3)*, trans. Loeb Classical Library.

Quinn, J. D., *The Letter to Titus*. The Anchor Bible (New Haven, NJ: Yale University Press, 1990).

Ramsay, W. M., *St Paul the Traveller and Roman Citizen* (London, Hodder and Stoughton, 1942).

Sanders, I. F., *Roman Crete: An Archaeological Survey and Gazetteer of Late Hellenistic, Roman and Early Byzantine Crete* (Warminster, UK: Aris & Phillips, 1982).

Schaeffer, F. A., *The Great Evangelical Disaster* (Westchester, IL: Crossway, 1984).

———, *The Complete Works of Francis A. Schaeffer: A Christian Worldview*, second edition, 5 volumes (Wheaton, IL: Crossway, 1982).

Spicq, C., *Theological Lexicon of the New Testament* (Peabody, MASS: Hendrickson, 1994).

The Strongest NASB Exhaustive Concordance (Grand Rapids: Zondervan, 2000).

Scott, E. F., *The Pastoral Epistles*. The Moffatt New Testament Commentary (London: Hodder and Stoughton, 1936).

Thielman, F., *Romans*. Zondervan Exegetical Commentary Series on the New Testament (Grand Rapids: Zondervan 2018).

Towner, P. H., *1-2 Timothy and Titus*. IVP New Testament Commentary Series (Downers Grove, IL: InterVarsity Press Academic 1994).

– – –, *The Letters to Timothy and Titus*. New International Commentary on the New Testament (Grand Rapids: Eerdmans, 2006).

Travis, S. H., *Eschatology* in S. B. Ferguson and D. Wright (editors), *New Dictionary of Theology* (Leicester: Inter-Varsity Press, 1988).

– – –, *Hope* in S. B. Ferguson and D. Wright (editors), *New Dictionary of Theology* (Leicester: Inter-Varsity Press, 1988).

Twomey, J., *The Pastoral Epistles through the Centuries*. Blackwell Bible Commentaries (Chichester: Wiley-Blackwell, 2009).

Wall, R. W. with R. B. Steele, *1& 2 Timothy and Titus*. The Two Horizons New Testament Commentary (Grand Rapids: Eerdmans, 2012).

Wallace, D. B., *Greek Grammar Beyond the Basics* (Grand Rapids: Zondervan, 1996).

Westermann, W. L., 'The Slave Systems of Greek and Roman Antiquity,' *Memoirs of the American Philosophical Society* 40 (New York: Noble Offset Printers, 1955).

Wieland, G. M., 'Roman Crete and the Letter to Titus.' *New Testament Studies* vol. 55, no. 3 (2009): 338-54.

Williams, P. J., A. D. Clarke *et al.* (editors), *The New Testament in its First Century Setting: Essays on Context and Background in Honour of B. W. Winter on His 65th Birthday* (Grand Rapids: Eerdmans, 2004).

Wright, N. T., *Paul for Everyone: The Pastoral Letters, 1 and 2 Timothy and Titus* (Louisville, KY: Westminster John Knox, 2004).

Yarbrough, R. W., *The Letters to Timothy and Titus*. Pillar New Testament Commentaries (Grand Rapids: Eerdmans, 2018).

Zehr, P. M., *1 & 2 Timothy, Titus.* Believers Church Bible Commentary (Scottdale, PA: Herald Press, 2010).

Zerwick, M. & M. Grosvenor, *An Analysis of the Greek New Testament*. vol. 2 (Rome: Biblical Institute Press, 1979).

Scripture Index

Old Testament

New Testament

Subject Index

AUTHOR INDEX

GREEK TEXT OF *TITUS*

Chapter 1

1. παῦλος δοῦλος θεοῦ, ἀπόστολος δὲ ἰησοῦ χριστοῦ κατὰ πίστιν ἐκλεκτῶν θεοῦ καὶ ἐπίγνωσιν ἀληθείας τῆς κατ᾽ εὐσέβειαν
2. ἐπ᾽ ἐλπίδι ζωῆς αἰωνίου, ἣν ἐπηγγείλατο ὁ ἀψευδὴς θεὸς πρὸ χρόνων αἰωνίων,
3. ἐφανέρωσεν δὲ καιροῖς ἰδίοις τὸν λόγον αὐτοῦ ἐν κηρύγματι ὃ ἐπιστεύθην ἐγὼ κατ᾽ ἐπιταγὴν τοῦ σωτῆρος ἡμῶν θεοῦ,
4. τίτῳ γνησίῳ τέκνῳ κατὰ κοινὴν πίστιν· χάρις καὶ εἰρήνη ἀπὸ θεοῦ πατρὸς καὶ χριστοῦ ἰησοῦ τοῦ σωτῆρος ἡμῶν.
5. τούτου χάριν ἀπέλιπόν σε ἐν κρήτῃ, ἵνα τὰ λείποντα ἐπιδιορθώσῃ καὶ καταστήσῃς κατὰ πόλιν πρεσβυτέρους, ὡς ἐγώ σοι διεταξάμην,
6. εἴ τίς ἐστιν ἀνέγκλητος, μιᾶς γυναικὸς ἀνήρ, τέκνα ἔχων πιστά, μὴ ἐν κατηγορίᾳ ἀσωτίας ἢ ἀνυπότακτα.
7. δεῖ γὰρ τὸν ἐπίσκοπον ἀνέγκλητον εἶναι ὡς θεοῦ οἰκονόμον, μὴ αὐθάδη, μὴ ὀργίλον, μὴ πάροινον, μὴ πλήκτην, μὴ αἰσχροκερδῆ,
8. ἀλλὰ φιλόξενον, φιλάγαθον, σώφρονα, δίκαιον, ὅσιον, ἐγκρατῆ,
9. ἀντεχόμενον τοῦ κατὰ τὴν διδαχὴν πιστοῦ λόγου, ἵνα δυνατὸς ᾖ καὶ παρακαλεῖν ἐν τῇ διδασκαλίᾳ τῇ ὑγιαινούσῃ καὶ τοὺς ἀντιλέγοντας ἐλέγχειν.
10. εἰσὶν γὰρ πολλοὶ [καὶ] ἀνυπότακτοι, ματαιολόγοι καὶ φρεναπάται, μάλιστα οἱ ἐκ τῆς περιτομῆς,

11. οὓς δεῖ ἐπιστομίζειν, οἵτινες ὅλους οἴκους ἀνατρέπουσιν διδάσκοντες ἃ μὴ δεῖ αἰσχροῦ κέρδους χάριν.
12. εἶπέν τις ἐξ αὐτῶν, ἴδιος αὐτῶν προφήτης, κρῆτες ἀεὶ ψεῦσται, κακὰ θηρία, γαστέρες ἀργαί.
13. ἡ μαρτυρία αὕτη ἐστὶν ἀληθής. δι᾽ ἣν αἰτίαν ἔλεγχε αὐτοὺς ἀποτόμως, ἵνα ὑγιαίνωσιν ἐν τῇ πίστει,
14. μὴ προσέχοντες ἰουδαϊκοῖς μύθοις καὶ ἐντολαῖς ἀνθρώπων ἀποστρεφομένων τὴν ἀλήθειαν.
15. πάντα καθαρὰ τοῖς καθαροῖς· τοῖς δὲ μεμιαμμένοις καὶ ἀπίστοις οὐδὲν καθαρόν, ἀλλὰ μεμίανται αὐτῶν καὶ ὁ νοῦς καὶ ἡ συνείδησις.
16. θεὸν ὁμολογοῦσιν εἰδέναι, τοῖς δὲ ἔργοις ἀρνοῦνται, βδελυκτοὶ ὄντες καὶ ἀπειθεῖς καὶ πρὸς πᾶν ἔργον ἀγαθὸν ἀδόκιμοι.

Chapter 2

1. σὺ δὲ λάλει ἃ πρέπει τῇ ὑγιαινούσῃ διδασκαλίᾳ.
2. πρεσβύτας νηφαλίους εἶναι, σεμνούς, σώφρονας, ὑγιαίνοντας τῇ πίστει, τῇ ἀγάπῃ, τῇ ὑπομονῇ.
3. πρεσβύτιδας ὡσαύτως ἐν καταστήματι ἱεροπρεπεῖς, μὴ διαβόλους μὴ οἴνῳ πολλῷ δεδουλωμένας, καλοδιδασκάλους,
4. ἵνα σωφρονίζωσιν τὰς νέας φιλάνδρους εἶναι, φιλοτέκνους,
5. σώφρονας, ἁγνάς, οἰκουργοὺς ἀγαθάς, ὑποτασσομένας τοῖς ἰδίοις ἀνδράσιν, ἵνα μὴ ὁ λόγος τοῦ θεοῦ βλασφημῆται.
6. τοὺς νεωτέρους ὡσαύτως παρακάλει σωφρονεῖν·
7. περὶ πάντα σεαυτὸν παρεχόμενος τύπον καλῶν ἔργων, ἐν τῇ διδασκαλίᾳ ἀφθορίαν, σεμνότητα,
8. λόγον ὑγιῆ ἀκατάγνωστον, ἵνα ὁ ἐξ ἐναντίας ἐντραπῇ μηδὲν ἔχων λέγειν περὶ ἡμῶν φαῦλον.
9. δούλους ἰδίοις δεσπόταις ὑποτάσσεσθαι ἐν πᾶσιν, εὐαρέστους εἶναι, μὴ ἀντιλέγοντας,

10. μὴ νοσφιζομένους, ἀλλὰ πᾶσαν πίστιν ἐνδεικνυμένους ἀγαθήν, ἵνα τὴν διδασκαλίαν τὴν τοῦ σωτῆρος ἡμῶν θεοῦ κοσμῶσιν ἐν πᾶσιν.
11. ἐπεφάνη γὰρ ἡ χάρις τοῦ θεοῦ σωτήριος πᾶσιν ἀνθρώποις,
12. παιδεύουσα ἡμᾶς ἵνα ἀρνησάμενοι τὴν ἀσέβειαν καὶ τὰς κοσμικὰς ἐπιθυμίας σωφρόνως καὶ δικαίως καὶ εὐσεβῶς ζήσωμεν ἐν τῶ νῦν αἰῶνι,
13. προσδεχόμενοι τὴν μακαρίαν ἐλπίδα καὶ ἐπιφάνειαν τῆς δόξης τοῦ μεγάλου θεοῦ καὶ σωτῆρος ἡμῶν ἰησοῦ χριστοῦ,
14. ὃς ἔδωκεν ἑαυτὸν ὑπὲρ ἡμῶν ἵνα λυτρώσηται ἡμᾶς ἀπὸ πάσης ἀνομίας καὶ καθαρίσῃ ἑαυτῶ λαὸν περιούσιον, ζηλωτὴν καλῶν ἔργων.
15. ταῦτα λάλει καὶ παρακάλει καὶ ἔλεγχε μετὰ πάσης ἐπιταγῆς· μηδείς σου περιφρονείτω.

Chapter 3

1. ὑπομίμνῃσκε αὐτοὺς ἀρχαῖς ἐξουσίαις ὑποτάσσεσθαι, πειθαρχεῖν, πρὸς πᾶν ἔργον ἀγαθὸν ἑτοίμους εἶναι,
2. μηδένα βλασφημεῖν, ἀμάχους εἶναι, ἐπιεικεῖς, πᾶσαν ἐνδεικνυμένους πραΰτητα πρὸς πάντας ἀνθρώπους.
3. ἦμεν γάρ ποτε καὶ ἡμεῖς ἀνόητοι, ἀπειθεῖς, πλανώμενοι, δουλεύοντες ἐπιθυμίαις καὶ ἡδοναῖς ποικίλαις, ἐν κακίᾳ καὶ φθόνῳ διάγοντες, στυγητοί, μισοῦντες ἀλλήλους.
4. ὅτε δὲ ἡ χρηστότης καὶ ἡ φιλανθρωπία ἐπεφάνη τοῦ σωτῆρος ἡμῶν θεοῦ,
5. οὐκ ἐξ ἔργων τῶν ἐν δικαιοσύνῃ ἃ ἐποιήσαμεν ἡμεῖς ἀλλὰ κατὰ τὸ αὐτοῦ ἔλεος ἔσωσεν ἡμᾶς διὰ λουτροῦ παλιγγενεσίας καὶ ἀνακαινώσεως πνεύματος ἁγίου,
6. οὗ ἐξέχεεν ἐφ᾽ ἡμᾶς πλουσίως διὰ ἰησοῦ χριστοῦ τοῦ σωτῆρος ἡμῶν,
7. ἵνα δικαιωθέντες τῇ ἐκείνου χάριτι κληρονόμοι γενηθῶμεν κατ᾽ ἐλπίδα ζωῆς αἰωνίου.
8. πιστὸς ὁ λόγος, καὶ περὶ τούτων βούλομαί σε διαβεβαιοῦσθαι, ἵνα φροντίζωσιν καλῶν ἔργων

προΐστασθαι οἱ πεπιστευκότες θεῷ. ταῦτά ἐστιν καλὰ καὶ ὠφέλιμα τοῖς ἀνθρώποις·

9. μωρὰς δὲ ζητήσεις καὶ γενεαλογίας καὶ ἔρεις καὶ μάχας νομικὰς περιΐστασο, εἰσὶν γὰρ
10. ἀνωφελεῖς καὶ μάταιοι.
11. αἱρετικὸν ἄνθρωπον μετὰ μίαν καὶ δευτέραν νουθεσίαν παραιτοῦ, 11 εἰδὼς ὅτι ἐξέστραπται ὁ τοιοῦτος καὶ ἁμαρτάνει, ὢν αὐτοκατάκριτος.
12. ὅταν πέμψω ἀρτεμᾶν πρὸς σὲ ἢ τυχικόν, σπούδασον ἐλθεῖν πρός με εἰς νικόπολιν, ἐκεῖ γὰρ κέκρικα παραχειμάσαι.
13. ζηνᾶν τὸν νομικὸν καὶ ἀπολλῶν σπουδαίως πρόπεμψον, ἵνα μηδὲν αὐτοῖς λείπῃ.
14. μανθανέτωσαν δὲ καὶ οἱ ἡμέτεροι καλῶν ἔργων προΐστασθαι εἰς τὰς ἀναγκαίας χρείας, ἵνα μὴ ὦσιν ἄκαρποι.
15. ἀσπάζονταί σε οἱ μετ᾽ ἐμοῦ πάντες. ἄσπασαι τοὺς φιλοῦντας ἡμᾶς ἐν πίστει. ἡ χάρις μετὰ πάντων ὑμῶν.

Greek New Testament - Nestle-Aland 26th/27th edition

www.sacred-texts.com/bib/gnt/co2

www.ingramcontent.com/pod-product-compliance
Lightning Source LLC
Chambersburg PA
CBHW062136020426
42335CB00013B/1229
* 9 7 8 1 9 6 9 8 6 5 4 2 8 *